THE ABCs OF NARCISSISM

SOARING PAST TOXIC PARTNERS

MICHELLE WILLIARD HOFFER

ARS METAPHYSICA

an imprint of Sunbury Press, Inc.
Mechanicsburg, PA USA

ARS METAPHYSICA

an imprint of Sunbury Press, Inc.
Mechanicsburg, PA USA

For information about special discounts for bulk purchases, please contact Sunbury Press Orders Dept. at (855) 338-8359 or orders@sunburypress.com.

To request one of our authors for speaking engagements or book signings, please contact Sunbury Press Publicity Dept. at publicity@sunburypress.com.

ISBN: 978-1-62006-085-8 (Trade Paperback)

FIRST ARS METAPHYSICA EDITION: October 2018

Product of the United States of America
0 1 1 2 3 5 8 13 21 34 55

Set in Bookman Old Style
Designed by Crystal Devine
Cover by Lawrence Knorr
Edited by Lawrence Knorr

Continue the Enlightenment!

CONTENTS

SO YOU KNOW . . .

■ I am not a doctor, or a psychiatrist, or a psychologist. This book is not a primer for diagnosis. As you will see, I do not attempt to provide clinical definitions in the vocabulary. I am someone who has been involved in an undiagnosed narcissistic relationship. Even though it was undiagnosed, it was extremely toxic nonetheless. No one should remain, endure, put up with, or deal with anyone who makes you feel sad, bad, or inferior on a regular basis in a systematic and methodical way.

■ The narcissist, the abuser, or the toxic person is both male and female. Narcissists are not only men. Toxicity runs in both men and women. Abusers can be either a man or a woman. The pronouns I use in this book to refer to the narcissist are male pronouns (he, him) for ease of fluency while reading instead of using he/she or him/her when reading. This is not a male-bashing book. (This is a narcissist exposing and abuser awareness book.) There are narcissistic wives, mothers, sisters, daughters, bosses, co-workers, clergy, fathers, brothers, sons, cousins, and so on.

■ When I was in an abusive relationship, I would scour resource materials to learn how to "be better." I thought "being better" for my abusive spouse was "self-improvement." I tried so many things to "improve." I was a gerbil on a wheel that was never going to truly meet the standards of his "improvement" while systematically being groomed for a lifestyle of worry, anxiety, and being grateful for those breadcrumbs he threw my way.

■ This book is meant to validate the red flags you are feeling in a toxic relationship, and to help you realize what might be happening to you by the predator who is disguised in soft, dreamy, fluffy sheep's clothing. It is my purpose to teach you that while the many traits and characteristics that follow in this book may occur in someone you love or care about, you are not trained to "fix" him. Only a specially trained mental health professional is qualified to treat the narcissist. Treatment requires long-term (and I cannot stress this point enough) very **long-term** therapy.

■ Each vocabulary word to describe the narcissist can be greatly expounded upon. The descriptions in this book are general explanations made by me from my own experiences and research. None of the descriptions are meant to diagnose or define diagnostically in any way. They are meant to validate the victim, to give the victim a wakeup call, and to encourage the victim involved in a toxic and abusive relationship to seek help.

■ Some of the vocabulary words use "everyone," "always," or "never" in the descriptions. They are generalizations of what it felt like for me when I was in a long-term relationship with someone who is narcissist-like.

■ While most descriptions provide a snippet of the tactic or manipulation used by the narcissist, also included are personal reflections and some tongue-in-cheek comments. (Again, I'm not a doctor and this is not a diagnostic tool.)

■ There are many repeated words in the descriptions. It is my hope to make it crystal clear to the reader that a relationship with a toxic person is not a healthy or balanced one. It is one that will leave the person feeling anxious, sad, depressed, and even suicidal. A narcissist-like individual is a twisted person. I must also stress, you cannot fix the narcissist or any toxic person. The layperson is not equipped to do so, regardless of how big your heart is or how much you think you love him, and/or want to help him. You cannot do this. The only person you can fix is yourself so you don't fall prey to another toxic individual again.

■ My advice to anyone who suspects they are involved with a narcissist: go no contact, seek help to improve your self-esteem, and for narcissistic abuse syndrome.

NATIONAL DOMESTIC ABUSE HOTLINE
1-800-799-7233

INTRODUCTION

■ Narcissism is a dangerous, twisted, and mean personality trait. While the male pronouns of "he" and "him" are used, make no mistake about it, there are female narcissists as well. The female narcissists just as twisted and manipulative as their male counterparts. There is a difference between the things a normal, well-adjusted person does in a relationship and the skewed ways these seemingly normal things are handled by a narcissist. The narcissist takes most any of the things mentioned in this book and will point the finger at you . . . saying you did this, YOU are a narcissist. (The narcissist will try to convince you that you are a narcissist, and you are the sum total of the relationship's problems.) This book is intended to be used by victims who need validation of what it is they are going through while with a narcissist, someone they think is a narcissist, a toxic person, an abusive person, or is simply just a jerk. (There is a reason the person is a jerk and it is not for you to figure out or to fix. Your job is to heal yourself and to become your best version of yourself.)

■ BE CAUTIOUS, if someone you suspect is a narcissist, toxic, or abusive, and that person has this book, they will likely use it to reinforce their agenda against you in your already low self-esteem, self-hating, self-blaming state. If anyone does that to you, THAT PERSON IS TOXIC! Leave him and seek help to rebuild your esteem and confidence. You are worth so much. Being in this vulnerable and raw state is temporary as you have given your power away, given your respect away, given your self-confidence away, and given your self-worth away to another person. Never do that again. This is a temporary state and you will gain your strength and empowerment back. (I will help you!)

■ Like most victims of narcissistic abuse, I was drawn to a narcissist because of prolonged exposure to a narcissist in my life who was supposed to be a role model of healthy love. This person is also, I believe, an undiagnosed narcissist. One only needs to look beyond the polish and perfection to see the clues of the real self-absorbed nasty, scary behaviors to see the real insecurity of the person. I tried to "please" this narcissist to no avail. I never measured up or was good enough to be loved by this person in my life. I met the man who would be my husband. He was charming and vibrant . . . just like my role model of love was. My life went from trying to please the person I looked up to, respected, loved and trying to make that person happy with me and see value in me, to trying to please my husband and trying to make him happy and to see the value in me. Thirty years later, along with many narcissistic episodes including rage, physical abuse, property damage, financial control, withholding of affection, triangulation, affairs, belittling, baiting and bashing, and so on . . . he announced, in front of a therapist, he never loved me. Never. Not at all during the 30 years had we known each other. I was shocked and of course, did not believe it. I thought I would need to try harder. Try harder. The only thing that happened was the abuse became more frequent. Here is an important piece I learned through my experience, therapy, research, and interviews: narcissists do not love others. The narcissist has a bizarre love-hate relationship with himself.

■ Following a 30-year marriage to an abusive man who has traits on the continuum of an undiagnosed covert narcissist, I suffered from PTSD, and narcissistic abuse syndrome. I was shell-shocked. He had yet another affair. This one was with a married co-worker of his with whom he worked closely. They told me they were "best friends." I believed them. I was conditioned to believe him . . . even when I didn't. For the most part, though, I believed him that they were friends. I was wrong. The beatings increased the longer their relationship continued and apparently deepened. He wanted me out of our home. While his initial strategic move was successful because I was totally blindsided, the remainder of the divorce proceedings further exposed who he really is and the type of human being that lurks in his body. From the divorce, he won someone else's wife. I won approximately 62% of his retirement, the assets, and equitable distribution, including alimony, PTSD recovery, a greater understanding of who I was and who I am now, and empowerment. With the shackles broken, I am SOARING!

■ The contents of this book are things I would tell a friend, family member, or someone I care about if they described any of the situations I use in the book. My advice to anyone who reads this book is this: protect yourself by going no contact from the abuser. Never ever, under any circumstances, contact this person again. If you have children with the abuser, there are safe email sites that are set up through the courts in which to exchange information about the children—only the children. The narcissist will never ever change. Narcissists can hide who they are for periods of time, but it does not last forever and the narcissist will be revealed. Again, the narcissistic abuser will never change. Therefore, you must go no contact. The narcissist in your life does not love you, value you, or care about you. The narcissist in your life regards you only as another inanimate object. The narcissist does not care about your feelings at all. The narcissist does not have feelings of empathy or compassion; therefore, the narcissist cannot and will not ever be able to give you love, empathy, or compassion in return. The narcissist is a selfish, self-centered monster who only thinks of himself and will easily discard you.

■ Are you a narcissist? More appropriately, has a narcissist convinced you that you are a narcissist? Or accuse you of being a narcissist? They are clever. They will project their insecure feelings and their negative attributes and behaviors onto you. They are masters at blame-shifting: blaming YOU for their choices. They are expert blame-shifters. So, it's highly likely YOU are not a narcissist. It is more likely that your relationship partner is the monster. Get out now! Seek help! Go no contact! Change your passwords, credit cards, email if necessary, and phone if necessary. Block him from all social media. (Block his friends from social media as well. They are not your friends anyway; so why keep them on any friends' list? You will make new friends.)

■ You are not alone. Share your story because together we are stronger.

#abusersabuse

NATIONAL DOMESTIC ABUSE HOTLINE
1-800-799-7233

THE STORY OF NARCISSUS
(BOTH ROMAN AND GREEK NARCISSUS MYTHS EXIST.)

In ancient times, there was a girl nymph named Echo who was unable to speak her own words due to a spell that was placed upon her by her mistress Goddess Hera. Echo could only repeat the words she heard.

There was also a vain boy named Narcissus. Early in his childhood, he became very pompous, arrogant, and even rude. He looked down on others. He often mistreated his friends and manipulated them for his own benefit. Narcissus grew into a handsome young hunter. Narcissus had many suitors and admirers. He had disdain and disgust for all those who would be attracted to him. In his opinion, the only one he believed that mattered, no one Narcissus met was good enough for him.

One day as Narcissus walked through the forest, Echo saw him. Echo immediately fell in love with Narcissus. Being unable to speak her own words to tell him how she felt, she followed adoringly after Narcissus for a while hoping to find a way to let him know how she felt. She wanted to be heard by him.

Narcissus realized someone or something was following him. He called out, "Who's there?" Echo replied, "Who's there?" After several repeating of Narcissus's last words, Echo wanted to reveal herself to the man she loved but she was afraid to do so. Narcissus demanded, "Come to me!" With that, Echo began to run to Narcissus. Echo, also said, "Come to me!"

Echo ran to embrace her love, Narcissus. Narcissus stopped her. He said, "Never will I love you." Echo repeated, "I love you." He told her to leave him alone. Echo repeated, "Alone . . . alone . . ."

Discarded by what Echo believed was her true love, Echo was devastated. She felt embarrassed and humiliated. She ran away . . . alone. She ran to the mountains to hide heartbroken and ". . . alone." Because "alone" was the last word she heard, it would be the last, and only, word Echo would ever be able to say. She never recovered from Narcissus's cruel rejection. Echo's existence was lonely. She quickly withered away to dust with only her voice remaining into perpetuity. (This is why you can hear the last words you yell into a mountain range: it is Echo returning your call.)

Goddess Hera found out what happened between her nymph, Echo, and Narcissus. Goddess Hera summoned Nemesis, the Goddess of Revenge to place a curse on Narcissus. Goddess Nemesis learned that Narcissus treated others around him with contempt and a dismissive attitude because of his proud and boastful ways. Nemesis saw how Narcissus did not return the love he took from others. She observed that he was not grateful for the precious gift of love nor did he appreciate it. Goddess Hera demanded Narcissus never be able to have love with anyone else.

And so, it would be that Nemesis cursed Narcissus with falling in love only with himself.

Nemesis decided to punish Narcissus by luring him to a pond where he saw his reflection. Narcissus was instantly in love with his own reflection. Narcissus was so enamored with his own reflection that he couldn't pull himself away from himself. He leaned into the pond. Every time he tried to touch, or kiss, the love of his life (his own reflection in the water), the reflection disappeared. He could not touch his reflection for fear of not being able to see it. He did not leave the reflection. He was obsessed. Narcissus became so thirsty but did not drink the water for fear of losing his reflection. Ultimately, Narcissus died of thirst, alone and tortured, at not being able to reach the love he wanted.

One of the morals of this story is that Narcissus had a heart too small to love anyone else **more** than he loved himself which is a deadly sickness.

Another moral is the only love Narcissus will ever know is from the "echo" of his own voice.

Still another, poignant meaning is that had Echo known that it was Narcissus's own ego issue, and had stronger self-worth, she would have left that jerk alone and would have gone no contact.

WHY DID YOU STAY?

"Why did you stay?" That is such a rude, insensitive, and thoughtless question. Asking "why" is negative to the victim. It makes us, the victims, only feel worse. The follow-up questions are just as intrusively cruel: Was it for money? Was it because you couldn't support yourself? Was it because no one else would want you?

My response to you is, "Why are you asking?" Are you asking for the scoop? Do you want the dirt to take and spread around? Are you a flying monkey?

Unless you have been in an abusive relationship, you have absolutely no idea the emotional and mental games that the abuser plays on his target. For as many people who are abused, there are that many reasons why we stayed: denial, fear, children, lack of a supportive network, and so on. So that you never ask anyone else this again, here is the primary answer to that question: because ultimately, we surrendered our power when he chipped away at our self-worth.

It becomes difficult for us, the abused, to decide to want to leave. Forget about "how" to leave. We cannot figure that out on our own. The negative chatter in our minds that has been implanted there also keeps us chained to fear and to him.

Most all decisions are extremely difficult for us. The abuser has stripped us of our confidence and self-worth. He wants to feel superior at our expense. He has us right where he wants us: without self-worth and dependent. We are the abuser's pawn.

Stop asking why and start offering compassion, even if you don't understand or comprehend the "why" of the victim's reasoning. The target, or victim, needs love, real love. Abuse is not love. She hasn't been loved in a very long time.

We, the victims, are scared. The last thing we need is more judging, more belittling, more having to defend our reasons. The abuser and his toxic flying monkeys are already in the process of shaming. We do not need any more questions like that from those we turn to during our scariest, darkest time. While you may be well-meaning, we don't trust you in questioning us. We have been questioned and belittled to death by our abusers. Our self-worth has been eradicated. We have been in a relationship where we had to defend most everything we did. We don't want to defend ourselves to you, our support group. We are finally out of the relationship. Help us to heal rather than finding out the "why" of it unless we are talking about it. Then, be supportive. We want to release our emotions and feelings, and to work through them at our pace.

We are going to blame ourselves. We have been conditioned to do that. We need you to help us release blame. We did not deserve any of his mistreatment. Help us to realize that. Nurture us with your support. Instead of making us defend our actions to you, why don't you step in to provide love, unconditional support, and tell the toxic abuser and his flying monkeys to back off? Provide a protective, supportive, nurturing wall around us, the victims, from their abuse so we can heal and become stronger.

If you do not believe us about the abuse, the best thing you can do is to not be in our lives to make room for authentic, compassionate, unconditional support, and love from better-suited people. An unempathetic person said to me "no one believes you" and went on to place guilt, shame and belittling on me. It sent me into a tailspin and directly to my therapist who taught me about the flying monkeys. As it turned out, one person who group texted me that he did not believe me, was going through his own issue as his current wife (I'm not sure which one) had ousted him as an abuser. His two prior long-term relationships ended the same way. (No shock to me. He had all the ear markings.) He was taking his projections out on me (abusers do that). It was his issue and his wife he was spouting off on, not me. Abusers project. Abusers abuse. Damaged people want to hurt other people. Hurt people want to hurt people. My reaction to him was nothing. He's an abuser with anger issues. His uncaring, uncompassionate comment showed me who he truly was had I had any question in my mind previously. I let him fade to black. To him, and others like him, I say "thank you" for you have made me strong. You have set me free so I can soar. Abusers abuse.

Another person wanted to phone me to talk. I answered the call thinking this person was a spiritual, kind-hearted person. It was a trick. She berated me while I was at my most raw, weak, vulnerable, scared state. She was so mean, so cruel. She had her flying monkeys agree with her. Is she a narcissist? Perhaps. Do I care? Not at all. I let her walk. As T.D. Jakes would say, "I gave her the gift of goodbye." It was sad, but it needed to be that way. I wasn't strong enough to deal with the nonsense. I surrounded myself with nurturing people who genuinely care about me. I let all others walk and fade to black.

Anyone who is cruel, or unkind to you, or leaves you during your most dire time is not worth being in your life. Do not struggle to prove to them who you are. Do not beg them to hear you or understand you. No way. Let them walk. You need only kind, loving, unconditional people in your life.

It will not be until you, the victim, are strong enough to see how much better your life is without these toxic abusers, and without the toxic takers that you will begin to soar. You will be FREE! You will be free from your abuser's control. You will be free from image management. You will be free from denial. You will be free from the flying monkeys. You will be free to SOAR!

#abusersabuse

NATIONAL DOMESTIC ABUSE HOTLINE
1-800-799-7233

VARIABLES—A MEASURE ON A SLIDING SCALE

■ **Continuum** – A measure of some sort with two opposing points or labels with varying degrees of measurement between points. Point A is a low degree on the measurement which is acceptable or manageable, to an extreme societal issue in which victim's lives are destroyed.

■ **Clusters** – Personality disorders are grouped using similar traits and variables.

■ Features and traits are used to help trained mental health professionals diagnose the personality disorder.

■ **Disorder** – A personality disorder is deeply rooted opposing the standard to society's standards in behaving, thinking (inner experience), feeling that causes distress, anxiety, pain, or problems functioning with others that are diagnosed by mental health physicians.

■ **Diagnosis** – Trained mental health professionals (psychiatrists and psychologists) are the most qualified medical professionals to diagnosis a person with any type of personality disorder, including narcissistic personality disorder (NPD).

■ Narcissist's, diagnosed or undiagnosed, and toxic individuals are both men and women. Once again, I am informing you that I use the male pronoun in this book. Toxicity, as well as personality disorders, are most definitely found in females as well. The females who behave in a toxic and/or narcissistic manner are just as cruel.

#abusersabuse

NATIONAL DOMESTIC ABUSE HOTLINE
1-800-799-7233

THE NARCISSIST

(THIS IS WHAT DOCTORS, PSYCHIATRISTS, AND PSYCHOLOGISTS USE TO DETERMINE NPD. I'M NOT A DOCTOR.)

■ Psychological standards for narcissism are listed below. (As stated earlier, I'm not a doctor, psychiatrist, or psychologist. The following is taken from the primer of mental disorders, and that is the one and only "American Psychiatric Association's Diagnostic and Statistical Manual of Mental Disorders"):

■ Narcissistic personality disorder (NPD) is a mental disorder found in both males and females. Those diagnosed with NPD have an **exaggerated** sense of self-worth and self-importance, and an extreme need for admiration and adoration. Those diagnosed with NPD are incapable of having sincere empathy for others. Those with NPD portray an illusion of charm, self-confidence, and popularity. The illusion masks the lowest self-esteem that's incredibly fragile to the slightest sense of perceived criticism and questions.

■ Narcissistic personality disorder (NPD) is recognized in the American Psychiatric Association's Diagnostic and Statistical Manual of Mental Disorders, Fifth Edition (DSM-5). The DSM5 is a diagnostic manual used by mental health professionals. Below are the nine traits of a narcissist, at least five of which must be present and continue for a substantial period, over various parts of life, for a diagnosis to be made. It is these nine categories from which this book is born.

1. Grandiose sense of self-importance.
2. Preoccupation with fantasies of unlimited success, power, beauty, or ideal love.
3. Sense of specialness, belief he can only be understood by or should associate only with other special or high-status individuals or institutions.
4. Need for excessive admiration.
5. Heightened sense of entitlement, leading to unreasonable expectations that others should treat him especially favorably or comply automatically with his expectations.
6. Tendency to be interpersonally exploitive. A person with NPD does not hesitate in taking advantage of others to meet his own needs and agenda.
7. Lack of empathy, an inability or unwillingness to recognize or identify with the feelings or needs of others.

8. An envy of other people, or conversely, a belief that other people envy him.
9. A tendency toward arrogant behavior or attitude.

(American Psychiatric Association, 2013).

#abusersabuse

NATIONAL DOMESTIC ABUSE HOTLINE
1-800-799-7233

THE NARCISSIST CONTINUED

■ **Narcissist** – I have read, interviewed, and researched extensively about Narcissistic Personality Disorder. I have learned there are two main types of narcissist, each of which has subcategories. I have had experience with people who resemble both types of narcissism. (Lucky me. I can relate.)

■ **The extrovert (overt) narcissist and the covert narcissist**—both are extremely manipulative.

■ Every narcissist, whether an overt narcissist or covert narcissist, have three exaggerated core traits: grandiose, excessive need for approval and admiration, and lacks empathy and compassion. The narcissist has no tolerance or concern for your needs if they are not aligned with his goals and agenda. You are only in the narcissist's life to fulfill a bizarre need, or narcissistic supply fix, for the narcissist. The narcissist does not love you . . . and never has. (My former husband told me that repeatedly. I was certain I "could do better" and then he would love me. That was a result of the grooming and conditioning.)

■ A narcissist requires victims to feed and stroke his ego and to completely support his beliefs (regardless of what they are). Like-mindedness is not expected; it is required. You won't truly or fully know this, though, until this person has you immersed in his life.

■ **Narcissist personality** – This person has, what seems to be from a victim's standpoint, split personalities. One personality that shows compassion, love, flexibility. (FYI—It is a false persona.) The other personality is extremely rigid, demanding, cold, calculating, and strategic. (This is who he really is.) The rigid personality is the dominant personality. It would appear the calculating personality is in control; while the flexible personality seems to be an illusion. Illusion meaning fake, pretend, manipulated, constructed. The flexible, loving, compassionate personality is an illusion, which means it was all an act. There are no split personalities with this person, there is only one: the one who uses any means necessary to feel superior over you by breaking your spirit to control and destroy you.

■ **Narcissistic fix** – The narcissistic fix is one of the narcissist's addictions. The narcissist must create havoc and turmoil in someone's life. The target of the narcissist's abuse is where the narcissist gets his fix. He relishes the drama and the pain he causes in someone else because this makes him feel superior. The narcissist also casts you as a pathetic individual for allowing him into your life (instead of appreciating you). The narcissist will never appreciate you.

■ **Narcissistic Personality Inventory** – An extensive inventory that measures the traits of a healthy self-awareness, self-esteem, self-confidence, assertiveness, spanning to arrogance, toward the irrational behaviors of a narcissist's rage, abuse, and control.

#abusersabuse

NATIONAL DOMESTIC ABUSE HOTLINE
1-800-799-7233

THE ABCs OF NARCISSISM

The alphabet that follows is a generic description of a narcissist. While this is not a diagnostic tool, this does explain the type of person from which you need to break free. The definitions are the types of responses I would give to a friend or loved one to help make them see the light if we were having coffee and conversation. There are so many additional words that could be used to describe the petty, cruel, cold-hearted behaviors of someone who is, or acts like, a narcissist.

This book will give you a sampling of the type of toxic person the narcissist is. At the core of someone who seems like they have Narcissistic Personality Disorder, or is a jerk, is control and emotional abuse of you. You do not deserve it . . . and you know it. If you are making excuses or justifying his behavior, stop doing that and seek help.

If you don't think anyone will love you, or you're not good enough, those are things the narcissist implanted in you into believing. It is not true. It will take time, but you will recover from the abuse. You will have an incredible healing when you are free. You will find incredible love when you are free. I promise you, there is light at the end of the tunnel. When you are through the tunnel, you will soar!

#abusersabuse

NATIONAL DOMESTIC ABUSE HOTLINE
1-800-799-7233

A

Abandonment – Narcissists have a fear of abandonment. The narcissist will purposefully trigger abandonment fears in you by disappearing on you, giving you the silent treatment, flaunting other women, triangulating, and sneaky around behind your back. The narcissist has a stable of "others" from which he can tag when he tires of you or wants to teach you a lesson. The narcissist will get rid of you before you can get rid of him. A narcissist will make the abandonment occur so he can be a righteous victim. The narcissist loves to turn the tables to be the (fake) righteous victim. (Oh, boo hoo, Mr. Narcissist!) Do not let the narcissist trick you or fool you. The narcissist is a manipulator who will abandon you, pull you back in, abandon you, pull you back in, and abandon you . . . and so on. This manipulation is called "hurt and rescue." Don't fall for it. The narcissist will never change. You are better than that. Go no contact from the narcissist to begin healing.

Abrupt – When the narcissist is ready to go, regardless of what else is going on around him or other people, the narcissist wants to leave that minute. It does not matter if you are relaxing, in a zone, having fun, finishing dessert in a restaurant, or in a conversation with him or someone else. It is all about the narcissist's wants, needs, and desires. This is rude behavior.

Abuse – The narcissist will abuse you at the beginning of your relationship, during your relationship, and after your relationship has ended. You need to know once the narcissist has started to tiptoe over boundaries, the narcissist is only going to continue slowly increasing with aggression. If the unkind, intolerable action has occurred (cheating, silent treatment, lying, stealing, physical contact, ignoring you, and so on), you better believe it will happen again or is still going on behind the scenes. It will not get better for you. You need to leave this relationship. It is not balanced. It is not healthy.

Abuse by proxy – The narcissist will enlist others help to hurt you, damage you, and abuse you. This comes in the form of friends, family, social media, attorneys, and police. The narcissist will turn his actions against you and will involve others to gaslight you, harm you, discredit you. This is all done as part of his need to dominate, win, and to feel superior against you. The narcissist wants to put you in your place. The narcissist wants to destroy your self-worth, confidence, and disempower you.

Abusive – Narcissists use many abusive tactics and abusive techniques to control others. Types of abuse the narcissist use include: emotional abuse, verbal abuse, mental abuse, physical abuse, sexual abuse, financial abuse. You need to leave this toxic relationship immediately. Go no contact. Seek help in recovering from narcissistic abuse.

Acceptance – The victim, the target of the narcissist, wants acceptance from people. You, the target of the narcissist, is a compassionate, loyal, empathetic person.

She will likely be a people pleaser in some way. Striving for acceptance makes the target vulnerable prey for the narcissist. You need to improve your confidence with some new activities, surrounding yourself with supportive, compassionate, and nurturing people, along with getting help from a therapist to improve your self-worth. You need only your acceptance . . . self-acceptance. You do not need to please anyone. Be your wonderful authentic self! (And go no contact from this jerk.)

Accountability – If you want the narcissist to take responsibility for something, anything: forget it. He may have called you a name, made fun of you, or ruined something important to you. He is not going to acknowledge it. It is not going to happen. The narcissist will go into an irate defensive mode when asking questions to him or of him. He will turn the tables on you. His negative behavior is always someone else's fault. The narcissist will spin any negative situation onto someone else. (Spinning and blame shifting are two of his superpowers.) He may even say you "deserved it" or that you "made him" do it. The narcissist will hide from being accountable, will use distractions and diversions from being accountable. Run, sweetie, run! Go no contact from him!

Accusatory – The narcissist will accuse you of many devious and uncouth acts including having affairs with young people, old people, men, women, gay, straight, lesbian . . . everyone. The narcissist is jealous of everyone. He believes everyone else has an angle; when, it is he who has the angle and agenda. Listen to what the narcissist is accusing you of doing. The narcissist is most likely doing the uncouth acts, and is blame shifting onto to you and placing you in a defensive mode. Do not play into this manipulative game of the narcissist. The accusations are meant to prove your loyalty to the narcissist which will begin a systematic type of isolation from your friends, work, and quite possibly your family. When the narcissist is unable to prove these bizarre accusations because they do not have any merit, he will double down on the accusations, blame, punishments, withholding love, silent treatment, and more manipulations until you apologize for you "making him think" these things about you. (Seriously? "Made him" think these things? You did no such thing. He is jealous and his behavior is out of whack.) When someone, any-one, starts accusing you of having affairs, or relationships where none exist, leave this jerk. I will tell you why: HE is probably projecting what HE is doing onto you. HE will get his righteous justification for doing what HE is doing by blaming YOU. (Does this sound twisted or confusing? It is. It is the mind of the toxic individual.)

Acknowledge –

■ The narcissist can spin an issue, especially one involving blame, onto someone else and will not acknowledge his part of the problem, or his mistake.

■ The narcissist takes credit for ideas not his and generally does not provide acknowledgment for a group collaboration.

■ The narcissist wants to be acknowledged for nearly every action he does . . . even when the action is something he "should" do. He wants constant credit and praise for participating in the relationship, work duties, or family activities.

Actor/Actress – The narcissist is an academy award winner. He can mimic actions that are appealing to you. The narcissist is a master of illusion in creating a charming persona . . . when he wants to do so. The narcissist turns it on and off like a bizarre light switch.

Addictions – Narcissists commonly have addiction issues, probably due in part to extremely low self-esteem. If he is in a long-term relationship, or mainstream position, he is a master at hiding his addictions. Make no mistake, the narcissist has at least one: fast cars, porn, fast women, loose women, married women, drugs, sex, alcohol, cars, body image, religion, and so on. My advice to you is to run! Run away and seek help for your own emotional wellness.

Adoration seeker – Everyone wants to be adored, treasured, and loved. The narcissist requires adoration without reciprocating it. If he is not adored, he will create havoc.

Adulterer – If the narcissist is married, you need to know that the narcissist does not love you, never has, and is cheating on you. As soon as you discover this, you need to leave the marriage before you catch something, endure more abuse, get cleaned out financially, or worse. The narcissist will not change. The narcissist will not improve with therapy. You are nothing to the narcissist. Get out now! Go no contact. If you have children, request that you and the narcissist only communicate through the safe parental email such as Family Wizard or one that the domestic relations department in your state offers. Go no contact except for the court ordered communication. Seek help for recovery from abuse.

Advice – The narcissist gives you his opinion, his advice, his suggestions, even when not asked, and expects you to follow it to the letter as if it were a demand. Obeying him and agreeing with him is a requirement. He believes that only his advice is the best. He is uncouth and will even say "I told you so" and remind you if something doesn't work out perfectly (which is normal and fine for normal human beings). Should a plan not go "just right" or "take a different but equally good" direction, the narcissist will find ways to discredit you and make you feel bad. If you hear the "advice," be prepared for an overload of mean underhanded or right in your face comments meant to attack your self-worth (not uplift you, elevate you, encourage you to try again, or give you support).

Afraid – Normal, well-balanced people are afraid of the narcissist they know. This is normal and not over dramatic. The narcissist has conditioned you to be afraid. Get away from this person as quickly as you can. The narcissist is toxic.

Agenda – The narcissist has objectives. He wants to destroy your self-esteem, emotionally destroy you, and to control you. The narcissist wants to make you his puppet who obeys him. He wants you to become the puppet he controls. He wants you to look only to him for guidance and direction. Then (and this is a typical narcissist), he will be disgusted by you because you are so pathetic. When you "don't know what to do next" because you have lost your sense of self, and because you gave him all of your power, he will kick you when you are down. The real narcissistic abuse "fun" is about to begin: mind-game time. The mind games are extreme and done in a manner that you do not even realize what is happening. My advice is to run! Run! Run! Get away from this terrible, selfish, self-centered, manipulative individual as fast as you can. Get help for emotional abuse. Mind games are no joke. You need support.

Agitator – The narcissist will create problems where none exist, will pick at a point until it's a full-blown issue. When you notice this, and the red flag goes off in your mind, you need to honor that instinct. The narcissist is a chronic agitator so get out now (as soon as you realize it happening).

Alienate – The narcissist will speak unkindly and accusatory of your friends and family. The narcissist will force you to take a side, a side that only he has created. He is planting seeds of doubt. The narcissist is strategically overtly or covertly alienating and isolating you from your friends and family.

Ambiguous – If you are confused, there is a reason. The narcissist is clever in having more than one meaning in conversations. He will then say you got it wrong or misunderstood (of course). The narcissist is purposefully unclear with plans, choices, and possible outcomes. Things are "not definite." The narcissist is "almost" making plans with you. Almost . . . but you're not quite sure because they were only implied. Be on guard . . . this is a trick, a tactic. You will be left sitting around wondering what to do. Waiting to hear from him. When you are first involved with the narcissist, the narcissist might take responsibility for one or two times of "getting it wrong" or "didn't think there was anything certain/definite planned." This is done to lull you into the web. It will shift. You will be accused and blamed for getting it wrong every time. Somehow not connecting will fall on your shoulders. When you realize the game this person is playing, get out of the relationship because the narcissist is not going to stop pulling this stunt.

Amplifies – If there is a tiny issue, you better believe in no uncertain terms, the narcissist will use this as an opportunity to make an issue greater than it needs to be. He does this to you to put you in your place, and thereby get his narcissistic fix by expressing anger and/or rage. Again, the initial issue may be minuscule or even nonexistent. The narcissist will exasperate the topic.

Anal retentive – To say that the narcissist is a creature of detail would be an understatement. The detail-oriented toxic individual focuses on the details HE wants or believes are important. There may be other more important details to attend to, but the narcissist wants what the narcissist wants. Something you may feel is important will be discarded by the narcissist because he didn't think of it. Or, the narcissist will take credit for it. Or, he will ignore what you say and then act as if he was the procurer of the idea due to his exceptional problem-solving skills. If you say that you just said the same thing, the narcissist will tell you that you are lying and act as if you are crazy, or will be annoyed that you are trying to take credit for "his" idea.

Anger issues – Narcissists seem fine, but there is an internal anger that seethes beneath the surface at all times. You never know what will set off a narcissist or trigger anger (quickly followed by rage). The anger outburst is generally in private as to not shatter the persona he has created with others. (This helps with his gaslighting efforts.)

Angles – Narcissists can read people. He knows who the empath is in the room. He knows who the people-pleaser is. He knows who is truly strong and confident. He can find a weakness and exploit it to suit his agenda.

Angry – The narcissist is always irritated and aggravated. You don't need that. Run, don't walk!

Answers – The narcissist is a master at avoidance. The narcissist will answer a question with a question, or a statement of fact he's made up as a question intentionally putting you on defense. The narcissist will seemingly supply an answer, but the words do not answer your question at all. It's an immature tactic the narcissist uses to appear superior and intentionally made you feel inferior. When this happens, the narcissist feels inferior, jealous, and angry about something but lacks the development and maturity to voice it without being mean so the narcissist will cut you down in this question manner.

Anxiety – The narcissist creates worry, fear, and confusion in his victims. The narcissist does this using lies and manipulations. The narcissist will lie about everything: big lies, little lies, easy to figure out lies. The narcissist doesn't care if you believe the lies or not. The narcissist cares about making you believe him. Making you, forcing you into a false belief. This anxiety producing game the narcissist plays reinforces the narcissist's fragile ego—making the narcissist feel superior. When the narcissist feels superior over you, the narcissist is then reinforced that you are not worthy.

Apology – The narcissist will never ever give you a **sincere** apology. You will receive the "sorry" words in a derogatory tone, angry tone, condescending tone. It will never be sincere. You will discover soon after the "apology" that it meant nothing, is insincere, as the narcissist will do the same things again. Almost immediately. You will also receive the non-apology in which the apology words may or may not be present, but blame on you most definitely is in the mix. You will never get a real apology from this jerk so don't try, wait, or hope for one. Instead, go no contact and never look back. The narcissist is toxic.

Argumentative – The narcissist wants to create problems to make you feel inferior, insecure, worry and doubt. The logic the narcissist uses during an argument is nonexistent. He is focused on winning at any costs. He will bring up old issues, make up new ones, and throw in things you had no idea occurred. The narcissist will use everything you say, or said in the past, against you. The narcissist will use a great deal of blame, manipulation, lies, fantasy stories, deflection, projection, and so on. The narcissist's warped bag of manipulation tricks knows no end. It is not wise to argue with someone who believes his own lies. You need to leave this relationship because it will not get any better.

Arrogant – The narcissist is self-important. Sometimes his arrogance is known. Other times, his arrogance is "shared" only with his target (behind closed doors).

He spouts off to his target at the "inefficiencies" of those he is jealous. Should you have success, the narcissist will take credit for it. His take on it might sound like, "I made you who you are!" "Without me, you're nothing." The covert narcissist is arrogant too. His sneak attack might sound snide, snarky, or pathetic/pitiful to undercut you. If you ask him about it, he will provide a number of BS excuses. Or, he will simply turn the tables on you and use it as an opportunity to sneak some ignorant comments to shred your feelings. Instead of talking about your feelings with a jerk or a narcissist, you need to ghost him. Block him on everything. Do not explain or answer him. This will only give the narcissist fuel to further blame you.

Attack – The narcissist will berate, criticize, or insult you for no apparent reason, as if out of the blue. You will be blindsided. There is a hidden agenda with the narcissist's attack. He is mad at himself for something or feels inferior for some reason. This reason may not even be in the attack. Suddenly there is verbal abuse (even if it is presented in a "calm" manner), and you have no idea why this is happening. Let me tell you, it's not you. It's him. He is throwing his venom at you, but it is all him. Your best defense: do not try to defend yourself against the narcissist's verbal assault. Just leave. Never look back. Do not make contact. Attacking and blindsiding is the narcissist's standard method of operation to throw you off balance.

Attention seeker – The narcissist is a validation seeker. He needs to be the center of attention. His jokes must be laughed at, or it's your issue. His ideas must be the best and implemented (by you – he won't do it), or he becomes angry and incensed. The narcissist must be the cleverest person in the room. The narcissist must be noticed for his behaviors, spirituality, ideas, suggestions, deeds, representation, and ethics. The list is endless. The narcissist wants attention—a lot of it. It doesn't matter if it's positive/good attention or negative/bad attention. The narcissist will seek attention from lies, stories, risky behavior, public accolades, illnesses (real, self-created, and imagined), emergencies (real, self-created, and imagined), and so on. If there is an opportunity to gain negative or positive attention, you will see the narcissist pushing you (and others) out of the way to get it. Bottom line: if the narcissist thinks you are not paying enough attention to him, or he is not the center of attention, he will create lies, diversions, and scenes to get the attention. Watch out. The narcissist is going to get it one way or another. See also "Outside attention."

Authoritarian – The narcissist is oppressive, dominant, and almost dictatorial. The narcissist treats you as a subordinate, unequal, as though you are less than. Regardless of wealth, position, power, gifts, once you hear, feel, or sense the authoritarian trait or personality, you need to turn and run and never look back. You must go no contact and seek help to work through narcissistic victimization and/or narcissistic abuse immediately.

Avoids –

■ Want to make plans? The narcissist plays a shell game with plans. He randomly throws several out and then will change them at will, sometimes not even telling you and then blaming you for getting it wrong.

■ Avoids accepting blame for all issues.

■ Avoids answering even the simplest of questions by deflecting or answering the question with a question (that is intended to throw you off balance).

■ Avoids commitments

■ Avoids following through.

■ Avoids decision making (but will take credit for good choices).

Awareness – The narcissist is not self-reflective and does not care to have any self-reflection unless it serves to improve his agenda. (See "Agenda.")

B

Back-handed compliment – It is very rare to receive a sincere compliment from the narcissist, let alone kind words to praise you. You will hear a nice remark wrapped up with an underlying mean comment. It is sneaky. You will hear the words. Then you will wonder, "Wait. What? What was just said to me and what did it mean?" Oh, I can tell you what it meant. He just made a fool of you. He just put you down in some way. Leave this sneaky snake.

Badger – The narcissist will repeatedly focus on a topic and/or question until he hears what he wants to hear. He will then continue with the focus, even after you give in, to cement his superiority as well as shame you for giving in so easily and perhaps not standing up for something, therefore, justifying his position even further.

Baffled – The narcissist will put you into a constant state of being confused (and most likely fearful as well). You will be baffled by the arrogance of the narcissist and by those who worship at the narcissist's feet. Let it go. Don't try to tell others who the narcissist really is. You need to protect yourself! Most likely the narcissist worshippers are narcissists themselves. Narcissists support each other in an odd dynamic.

Bait and bash – The narcissist is taunting you, manipulating you into reacting adversely, then the narcissist can claim victory over "exposing" YOU as the cause of drama, problems, fights, arguments. Baiting and provoking the victim by the narcissist is meant to divert attention away from the terrible things the narcissist does or has done. When you respond in a defensive, or sadly, a mind-lost response to the narcissist's constant battering, that's when the narcissist got what he wanted and will use it against you. It a blame-shifting bullying tactic that no one sees. They see the after effects with you as a person who is unstable. The narcissist tries to convince people into believing the victim is the aggressor. The bait and bash diversion tactic the narcissist uses proves one thing you must adhere: it proves the narcissist is dangerous, toxic, will do this again, and you must go no contact. Go no contact at the first sign of this type of behavior. The narcissist is clever and is a strategist. The narcissist will do this again . . . and again . . . and again if given the opportunity. Don't give the opportunity! Go no contact and seek help for narcissistic abuse.

■ Bait and bash will be used in many forms. Remember, the narcissist will use anything and everything you say and do against you. The narcissist will twist your words and gaslight you. Bait and bash are used to make you feel like you have no control, nothing left to lose and to make you look and feel crazy. I cannot stress this enough: you are not crazy. Once you are out from underneath the manipulation of the narcissist, you will discover how twisted HE is; and, how sane you are. Your time with the narcissist will seem like a nightmare from which you have awoken when you begin to gain your empowerment. It will be a breath of fresh air. You will need help healing from the narcissistic abuse.

Bait and switch – The narcissist uses this in the cycle with breadcrumbing. You will think he "finally gets it" and will treat you better. That was the bait. The narcissist will switch back into the degrading game with you quickly. That's the switch. Don't go back after you have broken up from that toxic relationship. The narcissist will destroy you emotionally.

Baller – The slang term means a person has money, is extravagant, is impressive, and has arrived at a higher social standing. While the narcissist may be an executive or performs well at his job, he is not a true baller. He is a fake. Even if he has a lot of money, a narcissist is, and will always be a wannabe baller. He is a wannabe because he will have to proclaim it for all to hear, "I'm a baller!" A real baller doesn't have to proclaim anything. A real baller just is. (The narcissist is more than likely in debt up to his eyebrows.)

Bank accounts – Do not let the narcissist anywhere near your bank account, your bank account numbers, your social security information, debit cards, and credit cards. Do not offer to pay for things the narcissist needs to be responsible for paying. (This includes his traffic tickets, child support, his credit cards, rent, mortgage, phone, utilities.) You are not responsible for the narcissist's bills. The narcissist will try to blame you for his lack of funds. He has enough money to run around and do all these things for himself. When it comes time to pay his bills, he will not have enough money. Or he will shower you with gifts and go out to love-bomb you and win you back. You are then paying for all his insanity if you open your wallet or give the narcissist your credit card to pay for the bills. The narcissist is not quick to pull out his wallet. There will be that awkward moment at the register where you will feel embarrassed. Do not take your wallet at all. Another favorite of the narcissist is to repeatedly "forget" his wallet when going out. The narcissist is intent on taking full advantage of you and your resources until they are depleted. Do not fall for this. Keep your wallet in your purse, at home, hidden. Go no contact from this "forgetful," user jerk. He is toxic.

■ If you are married to a narcissist, I would suggest watching the money closely. My former husband had a secret bank account into which he was funneling money. He also controlled the finances to "take care" of me. In thirty years, I never once did the banking. I did not have a credit card. I wasn't allowed to use the checkbook. (He kept that in his locked briefcase.) I did have an ATM card of which I did not know the pin numbers. I had to ask to use it. I received an allowance of $10 a week. Toward the end of the marriage, I had been given an increase of $20 a week. I could use that as spending money.

Basic needs – The narcissist threatens your very being, emotional health, and basic needs of food, shelter, clothing, love, and significance. If you feel diminished in any way and are afraid to bring it up to your partner because you "know what the outcome will be" then you need to leave the toxic relationship. If your basic needs are ignored or belittled, and you are afraid to talk to your partner about how you feel, this is not healthy for you.

Battered – The narcissist will clobber you mentally, physically, emotionally to make the narcissist feel better. You are nothing to the narcissist. Do not try to prove your value or worth to the narcissist. The narcissist cannot change his opinion of anyone. The narcissist will continue to batter you during the entire life of your relationship. It will end only when you go no contact and never speak, text, email the narcissist. Do not look for or at the messages from the narcissistic abuser. There is no reason to read his lies and manipulations. Go no contact. Get a protection from abuse if you fear for your safety.

Behave – The narcissist tells you how to behave either overtly or covertly using manipulations. You will have your personality stripped, and will be groomed to be under the narcissist's control. Should you fail to fully be under the narcissist's control, you suffer "the consequences" put forth by the narcissist. In a healthy relationship, you will be loved for you, your behavior, your likes and dislikes, your wants, and needs and you will be celebrated and embraced: not changed because you are lacking in an area or are not good enough. You are more than good enough.

Behavior – The narcissist's behavior will change from being loving and attentive (remember: you were his "everything"), to you feeling "a disconnect." Know that what you feel is real. It's what the narcissist does. The narcissist will blame-shift and tell you it is your behavior that has changed. The narcissist uses blame-shifting quite often.

Beliefs – You can believe this: the narcissist believes his own line of BS. Every fabrication and lie he tells, he will believe it and will attempt to make others (the flying monkeys) believe his baloney too.

Belittle – The narcissist will make you feel unimportant and unworthy using words and his tone. Your feelings, your actions, your attempts to please will be minimized and trivialized.

Benefit of the doubt – You will give in to the narcissist repeatedly . . . even when his stories change, you absolutely know he is lying, and your intuition tells you the narcissist cannot be trusted. You give the benefit of the doubt. He will not give it to you and will make up stories about you that you feel you must defend yourself and your character against. Don't bother. It will only get worse. Instead, turn and run and go no contact.

Berate – The narcissist will bully you into doing things. The narcissist will call you names for things you do or attempt to do. The narcissist's attack is an angry one.

Betrayal – One word: disloyal. There is very little, if any, loyalty from the narcissist. The narcissist will always be loyal to himself first. The narcissist will place blame on others should the narcissist's behavior negatively impact others. The narcissist will figure out a twisted way to blame others for his mistakes in claiming betrayal, or others "made" him do it.

Blame shifts – The narcissist will not take responsibility for his issues and/or problems. The narcissist will turn the focus away from what it was he did to you, to someone else, to another topic altogether. The narcissist will go so far as to totally place blame on the other person for something he did. This is an emotionally abusive tactic meant to confuse and instill self-questioning of the victim.

Blames – It does not matter if you are right, or wrong, or have no idea what the narcissist is talking about, YOU are to blame for whatever ails him.

■ If the narcissist loses something, you are to blame. A narcissist will blame you for the lost or misplaced item. A narcissist will blame everyone else for his lost or misplaced items. Not that there is necessarily blame or fault to be assigned because a mistake is a mistake, but, the narcissist will never admit to fault or error (even when the missing item turns up in the narcissist's own pocket). The narcissist will continue to lie and blame you. You will be blamed for taking it, moving it, or he "gave it to you." He will say you have whatever it is that is missing. Should he find the item, not tell you, and continue blaming you. Or lie about its reoccurrence. The narcissist will not take ownership of the lost item. He is above ever losing anything and never makes mistakes . . . only you, and others like you, lose things and make mistakes.

■ Should you find the item that you know you did not have and you know he's misplaced and is placing blame on you, this simply proves his theory you had whatever it was, you lied, and are covering up your maleficence by finding it.

■ A narcissist will lie or manufacture situations to make you look bad and will blame you for the situation. Ultimately, everything is your fault with a narcissist.

■ The abuser will say you are mean or are hurting his feelings by not doing whatever it is he wants you to do (when he wants it done). You will be blamed for not doing what he wants when he wants it done which is usually counterproductive to your wellbeing in some way. This is why the abuser wants you to do what he wants when he wants it as soon as he tells you so you do not have time to think it through. A fit, a temper tantrum, or narcissistic rage, will accompany his blame game.

■ Refer back to one: the narcissist never takes responsibility or ownership for anything.

Blindsided – Unexpectedly, out of the blue, the narcissist will begin a conversation to attack you or bait you (in an attempt to use the bait and bash technique). The narcissist will bring up a tough or controversial topic when you are in a happy or peaceful place to sneak attack you with his ambush. There is no preparation for his blindsiding behaviors. The narcissist loves blindsiding his victims . . . with a proverbial shovel to the back of the head. Yes, his surprise attacks are that cruel.

Blows things out of proportion – Oh geez. Pay attention because the world is ending.

Boastful – The narcissist thinks he can do anything, and he does not mind telling you all about it. A narcissist will live in the past of his glory days from his youth, sharing stories, awards, and pictures. This can be decades past; it does not matter to the narcissist because the narcissist is emotionally stunted. The narcissist will boastfully fill your hopes with empty promises.

Boiled frog – The parable is about a frog. If a frog is put into hot, boiling water, the intelligent frog wastes no time hopping out of the water to escape to safety. If a frog is placed in comfortable water, the frog will stay and enjoy the water. Ever so slowly and methodically, the temperature will be turned up degree by degree. The frog will not notice the change in temperature as the frog's body adjusts. The poor, little frog will not realize he is being boiled to death; and therefore, will not jump out of the pot to save his life. I felt like a boiled frog.

Bored – The narcissist will bore of you easily. You will wonder what happened. You will begin to gather some sense of stability when he returns because he will become bored with his new flavor. Then he will return to you . . . for a short period of time to create havoc and become bored again.

■ Because the narcissist enjoys drama, even though the narcissist says he doesn't, the narcissist will become bored easily. When things seem peaceful and calm (and you're relieved), that's about the time the narcissist will pounce to create some fun for himself at your expense.

Boss/Manager/Leader/Roles of authority – The narcissist as a boss with underlings or leader of a club/group loves the attention of being in charge. The narcissist may be given a leadership role due to the "charm" in the narcissist's personality towards the narcissist's superiors. The narcissist may not be qualified for the position but will lie his way to the position. The narcissist will blame underlings for failures. The narcissist will go through employees. The narcissist is not a leader in bringing people together (except the flying monkey praise adulators). The narcissist is damaging to whatever the narcissist is leading. The narcissist does not look at the big picture. The narcissist surrounds himself with "yes" people. The narcissists "advisors" will share information to the narcissist in his favor. The narcissistic leader will interpret most any information given to suit the narcissist's agenda and to fit into the model the narcissist wants. This includes facts, numbers, statistics, and so on that would seem otherwise concrete.

Bounce – Remember when the narcissist said he wasn't cheating on you? He will bounce to her as soon as he is ghosting you or has dumped you. Remember when the narcissist said he didn't have any money, and you go broke trying to build a future with him? The narcissist will suddenly go on trips, buy a house, and gifts for his new target. Remember when that was you? Well, be glad he is onto the next one. Go no contact. Do not let that creep back for more when he wants to return because he has depleted the next one. Seek help in rebuilding your self-esteem. Block him from everything. Change your passwords. Cancel your credit cards and order new ones. Never reply or respond to the creep ever again. He's done enough damage. (And no, he has not changed.)

Boundary breaker – The narcissist will discover your limits, things that are offensive, will never do, will not allow, and not say. He will then systematically set out to break your boundaries. If it is too difficult for him, he will badger and belittle you until he achieves his twisted goal. When you decline an offer, an invitation, or gift from the narcissist, if you are in the love-bombing stage, the narcissist will push your boundaries by putting you in the position to defend your reasoning why you are declining. This may be done in a playful manner. Or it could be done in an overt way. The narcissist knows how to instigate you to defend yourself. Here is the biggest tip: never ever defend your reasons for declining anything. You are entitled to self-preservation or to simply say "no thank you." Should you notice this pattern, it is time to leave him before it goes any further.

Brag – The narcissist will boast and gloat about himself or will want you to do it for him. The narcissist needs validation. Without anyone noticing all the good things he is doing or has done, he feels as though you (or people with you) are not fully enamored by him and are ungrateful, or ill-mannered, or uncouth because his greatness has not been recognized.

Brainwash – The narcissist is systematically brainwashing and conditioning you every opportunity he has. This begins with the first conversation he has with you to see if he wants you as his next victim. He wants to find out if you are weak, vulnerable in some way if you are easily led astray, and so on. The emotional abuse the narcissist creates in the victim is long lasting. Love bombing is the first step in his brainwashing technique. Your life will go from feeling like this fella really knows you and understands who you are with the love bombing to hell and an insurmountable amount of self-doubt created by the threats, belittling, badgering, physical abuse, critiquing, silent treatments, withholding of affection, and so on.

Breadcrumbing – Oh, your narcissist has seen the light. He's back to his wonderful self from the beginning of the relationship! He's once again the man you fell in love with. Ha. Nope. Wrong. It is a trick. This attention is short-lived. The manipulation the narcissist just pulled is called breadcrumbing. The narcissist gives you the slightest amount of attention to keep your interest in him going. He has no interest in you or in developing a meaningful relationship with you. Occasionally, the narcissist will give you a present, do what you want, be the person you thought he was. It's a trick. He's throwing you a bone to keep you interested in him. As soon as you think he is back to the loving guy you knew, bam . . . the real person shows up again pulling his stunts. This is all ego driven by the narcissist. It's cruel and is a total waste of your time, energy, and heart. It leaves you feeling spiny, confused, eats away at your self-esteem, and hurts emotionally. You are in a constant state of flux and wonder. If he must consider or make you wait while he decides if you're the person for him, then he ISN'T the person for you.

Break the shackles – To break the mental hold that the narcissist has on you, you need to go no contact and get help to heal. Do not contact the narcissist for any reason whatsoever.

Break up/Make up/Break up/Make up cycle – This is the game of the narcissist to see how far he can take you. Do not be fooled. He has not changed. He is still the smooth-talking wolf in sheep's clothing individual. Once you break up, leave it that way. You will feel lonely and maybe even remorseful for a period. That's natural, especially after the narcissist has infected your mind. Do not get back together. Go no contact. Give yourself some time to heal, hang out with friends, and go on dates. Do not contact or get back together with the narcissist or you are continuing the cycle and you do not want that!

Broken – The narcissist wants to damage you, wants you to feel empty, and wants you to feel as though you are broken. The narcissist wants to destroy your self-worth. The very best way to avoid these feelings is to leave the toxic person now. (If it's around the holidays, trust me, the narcissist has left you or creating some sort of pain for you. It's not worth it. He will do this for every holiday. It's what he does. HE is the empty, damaged, broken individual. Don't let him take you down into his dark pit.)

Brute – You cannot reason with a narcissist. Once something is manufactured in the narcissist's mind, he will blow that up into something it isn't. Like an animal, there is no reasoning with a narcissist. Like an animal, the narcissist can quickly go out of control with the manufactured thoughts he creates. A narcissist is brutish—a narcissist behaves badly. The brutish behavior can be verbal, mental, as well as physical. The narcissist is rude.

Bullheaded – The narcissist can appear to be "strong-willed" or "bull-headed." Have no doubt about it: a bully is a bully. A bully is relentless and unwilling to change . . . just like the misnamed "strong-willed" person. (And this is different from being strong and confident. Don't let the narcissist trick you when you show your confidence. Your confidence will be used against you by the narcissist.) Bullheaded, is a bull with a "y" at the end.

Bully – The narcissist intimidates people verbally, emotionally, mentally, and sometimes even physically. He is a bully, a coward, an abuser, a manipulator, and an individual with extremely low self-esteem.

C

Calling the shots – The narcissist wants to be the boss, the authoritarian of the relationship. He thinks this equals power, control, and respect. Does this sound like a dictator? It is. The narcissist wants the upper hand in the relationship and will take it by force and manipulation. This type of behavior is selfish, egomaniacal, and self-centered. Balanced relationships are healthy and fun. This is not one of those types of relationships.

Calling them out – The narcissist does not want to be called out and will react with insensitivity to rage if questioned or called out on a lie, getting caught in a lie or deceitful act, or any other mean manipulation. The narcissist will amp up his efforts after being called out to make you feel bad and convince you how wrong you are. He will lie and hold onto his lie and keep up with his lie rather than what an evolved, mature adult would do: acknowledge and apologize. The narcissist is not mature or evolved. The narcissist is selfish and self-centered. The amped-up efforts to trick you or force you, into submission of belief and even apology (just to get out of the narcissist's crazy making argument). This may seem like the narcissist is angry, but it is more a challenge to the narcissist. The harder the narcissist must work, the angrier the narcissist is. It has nothing really to do with you. You may apologize to make the rage stop, but the narcissist is not finished with you. It is silent treatment time. It is a mean, sick, twisted game. If you would rather not be a pawn in the narcissist's game, you must go no contact. Never ever contact the narcissist again for any reason whatsoever.

Calm – During the calm periods, after a narcissistic fix or argument, the calm period is when the actor appears.

Captive – The narcissist makes you his emotional prisoner. He requires your obedience.

Care – The narcissist does not care about you at all. The narcissist enjoys you paying attention to him. Other than that, there is nothing there for you. The narcissist is an empty shell who sees you as an empty vessel he could care less about. Make no mistake about it: the narcissist will mistreat you because he does not care about you. Leave the relationship right away. You are worth more than that.

Catfish – Either while with the narcissist, and likely when you have gone no contact, the narcissist, or his flying monkeys could create false social media accounts in an attempt to be your friend or new work contact. He wants to wreak havoc on your life. This is abuse. You must block him, his friends, his family, his co-workers, and anyone else you can think of that relates back to him in some way. You must be very careful when accepting new friend requests or contacts on any social media and dating platform. (See "Social media safety.")

Challenge – The narcissist enjoys conquests—especially the female variety. He sees you, and it does not matter if you are married, in a relationship, or some other "difficulty." If you live far away, he will convince you to move to him (then emotionally abuse you in person). He wants what he wants when he wants it and it does not matter to him how he will get it. The rules of society and decency to not matter to him. He will say and do whatever he needs to do to "win" you over to him. (Don't fall for it!) He is a chameleon who can change colors to get what he wants. He is using you for sport. You'll eventually realize this when he goes off and cheats with someone else. This will be your opportunity to realize what a terrible person he is, get out of the relationship while you can—before any more time passes you by with this creep. Go no contact and surround yourself with strong, supportive people who will aid in your recovery. (If anyone tries to hinder your recovery with unkindnesses, challenges, bringing up years ago, or judge you for any part of what you've been through, then let them go. You don't need that type of person in your life. Let them walk. You need only supportive, nurturing people.)

Chameleon – The narcissist reads the feeling of his environment so that is able to adapt to his surroundings. He changes who he is almost instantly and effortlessly. He needs to be the most interesting person in the room. Well, actually, he needs to have the most interesting persona in the place. Who is this person? He is the most inauthentic person in the room. You will never truly know him because he does not know who he is himself. Because he does not know who he is, he cannot be satisfied or fulfilled. He will take out all of his frustrations, anger, disgust, and disappointments out on you. You will be the receiver of his projected failings. He is a chameleon on the surface, but underneath he is a monster who wants to destroy you.

Change – The narcissist will never improve as a relationship partner or friend. Not now, not with therapy, not with your help. He is not introspective and doesn't want to be. He is so arrogant he will probably tell you that he will never change. He might even yell it at you. Believe him! He will never change. Never. Go no contact.

Chaos – Chaos is the narcissist favorite time. The narcissist operates better in chaos. He feels superior in chaos. He will create chaos, blame you and feels good about himself.

Character – This book describes the narcissist's character. The narcissist is devoid of true emotion. The narcissist is concerned only with himself. The self-absorbed attitude of the narcissist lacks true empathy for others. The behaviors and the characters of the narcissist can be explained in the following two sentences: What about me? How does this affect me?

Charisma – The narcissist appears to exude charm and people seem to flock to him. It's an illusion. The very first time you experience any red flags in your mind warning you that something isn't right, or the first time the narcissist makes you feel bad about yourself, turn and run and never look back. Do not contact the narcissist for any reason.

Charmer – At first, the narcissist is a delight to you and everyone around you. It's an illusion. Love bombing will quickly follow the initial meeting of the victim. Relationship steps move fast. This is a red flag!

■ Everyone will think the narcissist is so charming and wonderful, so nice, and even "gentle as a dove." People may even think he is a "saint." He's not any of those things! Let the others think what they want about him. He is toxic to YOU. Get out! Go no contact!

Chase – He wooed you nonstop in the beginning. Now the narcissist wants you yearning for him and chasing after him, his love, his attention, and affection. Seriously, leave this jerk. You should chase no one! If he does not want you, then he does not want you. Do not play his chasing game.

Chastises – The narcissist is mean. He will undercut you with tone, and words. The narcissist will chastise, or make fun of in a mean way, things you like, people you like to make you feel bad about yourself . . . as bad as the narcissist feels about himself. The narcissist will chastise you, your children, your family, your pets, your job, your religion, your income, and your way of life. The narcissist is an insecure, emotionally underdeveloped child in an adult's body. Turn and run. Go no contact!

Childish – The narcissist is immature. Remember in junior high when you got into a pre-teen 8th-grade argument with another girl? Or worse, remember in elementary school when you saw your classmate throw a temper tantrum? This is what it is like when the narcissist is unleashing his wrath on you or trying to throw you off balance. He does not make sense. The narcissist's emotional development is either nonexistent or stunted. The narcissist behaves like a big baby child in an adult's body. This is the narcissist's problem, not yours. The narcissist will try to make it your problem, and you may even want to nurture the narcissist. This is a big mistake. The narcissist will only be an emotional vampire to your good intentions. The narcissist will turn your help into darkness and bad attempts. The narcissist will use your kindness to chip away at your self-esteem and self-worth. When you first notice the childish behaviors, this is a red flag to your safety. Turn and run and go no contact!

Children – The narcissist will ignore either all or some of his children, pitting the "better" child against a victimized child. The narcissist parent will withhold love and affection. The child of the narcissist will never receive unconditional love— even the "favored child." The child of the narcissist will live a conditional childhood, even life if the child does not learn what appropriate relationships are made of. The narcissist parent is mean, unkind, and a saboteur to the child/children he does not like and will cut off the ones he does like just as quickly. The narcissist will not feel bad or remorse for anything the narcissist does against the child. The narcissist does not have empathy for anyone including the narcissist's own children. The child (this includes the adult child) of a narcissist is unreasonably expected to live the life the narcissist wants, behave the way the narcissist demands to the point of denying oneself. If the rules, standards, and expectations of the narcissistic parent are not met, the narcissist will blame the child and use various demeaning and belittling tactics to instill shame and guilt. This is likely to include physical abuse. The narcissist parent will make the child's life miserable for the child and anyone who gives the child positive attention. Any successes the child (adult child) has, the narcissist will take the credit for this success. In private, the narcissist will find something "wrong" with the achievement and will use this to belittle the child. Remember, it's all about the narcissist, the narcissist's needs, the narcissist's happiness—even the children do not escape from the narcissistic victimization. It may even be worse for the children because they are dependent on the narcissist. The children may not even know any better and will think this is normal interaction and standards of parents. A narcissist's relationship with his child/children is twisted as the narcissist will be unusually close and even possessive over the children (even the ones the narcissist does not find favor with). Narcissists are mean, threat makers, humiliations, punishers. The life of a child, including an adult child, of a narcissist is a dark, lonely, confusing place. The child, adult child, must get help to learn to cope.

Choices – You are not the narcissist's first choice for anything. You are not the toxic game-player's second or third choice. He has a "me versus you" mentality. You are the enemy (especially when he is angry about something . . . anything). He will choose other women, men, coworkers, friends, his mother, his father (even if they are abusive toward him), his children (even if they are your children as well), and strangers before he picks you, or defends you or your point of view. You are his last choice. You are last on his list.

Circular conversations – This is a manipulation to throw the victim off balance. It's a never-ending argument meant to break your spirit.

Circumstances – You will be blamed for all the bad behavior of the narcissist. You "make him" behave in a certain way. There's also the circumstances of the narcissist's life that he will blame his failings on. Unless, of course, he is blaming you for the circumstances. All circumstances that are not positive are someone else's fault. They are never the narcissist's responsibility.

Clingy – This is a favorite word of the narcissist. He wanted to be with you constantly. When he finally wins you over, he no longer wants you (unless it serves him). He will call you "clingy" often. He will tell you are "pressuring" him. He will make you believe you have turned into a clingy person. (This is a gaslighting tactic.) When he is onto his next fix and is juggling multiple partners, he keeps his victim confused and off footing so that the victim needs to contact him to find out "what is up?" The narcissist uses his special form of ghosting to convince his victims, as well as others, that you (the victim) are "clingy" and dependent on him. The narcissist will manipulate, or trick you, into believing you are clingy. The narcissist will provide evidence of how you intruded into his activities due to your clinginess. This is by design. You are not clingy. You liked the attention he was previously giving you because you were in a whirlwind relationship with someone you thought was upstanding and understood you. The narcissist most like created the persona of who you wanted. It was all a manipulation. You can break free from this by going no contact from the narcissist, and by seeking help from supportive, nurturing people. Do not give this jerk a second chance, a third chance, a tenth chance . . . or any chance. He will continue to do this type of drawing you in and then pushing you away behavior to hurt you.

Close minded – Right or wrong, the narcissist is unyielding in certain lines of thought. The narcissist is obsessive in proving his point. The narcissist is unlikely to ever change his opinion on topics because he is always right and everyone else is wrong. (It's everyone else who needs to change.)

Cluster B – Narcissistic Personality Disorder (NPD) falls under the Cluster B of mental illnesses along with Antisocial Personality Disorder, Borderline Personality Disorder, and Histrionic Personality Disorder. Cluster B disorders have interpersonal conflicts. YOU CANNOT FIX THEM! Only a person with a medical degree should work with a narcissist.

Codependency – A narcissist needs a codependent of the exact opposite to thrive. A codependent partner is a pleaser, a fixer, a helper, a person who sacrifices their own needs for that of the narcissist. The codependency has been groomed in you either by this narcissist or another before him . . . or perhaps several before him, and maybe even by a primary family member or members. If you are in a relationship or were in a relationship with a narcissist, chances highly probable are you are codependent. You may be looking to fill some need of your own—a "fix him"/" rescue him" issue. First, you cannot fix or rescue anyone; let alone a narcissist. Instead, you must seek therapy to strengthen your person, heal yourself, find yourself, and become empowered.

Coercive control – When someone uses threats, harassment, various forms of bullying, punishments, or force to make you do something: get out. This person has no respect for you. While it may be necessary to ground a child for misbehavior; with adult relationships, this is not appropriate. You and your partner need to be at the same level. One should not have more power than the other. If someone consistently tries to harshly persuade you into things you do not want to do, or go to events/places you don't want to go: get out of this relationship and seek help during your recovery following his abuse.

Cognitive distortion – The mind convincing someone that something is/isn't true or did/did not happen. Things that are rational and have a normal explanation become cognitive distortions to the narcissist. The cognitive distortions that play internally in the narcissist are let loose onto unsuspecting victims. The narcissist takes these normal activities or events and turns them into something that is purposefully meant to make the target feel bad. When this first happens to you, you will second guess yourself wondering if that, indeed, really was your unconscious meaning for it. This begins the narcissist's activity of chipping away at your self-confidence and self-worth. It's a trick. After it happens several times to you, you may catch on. The moment you catch on to this divisive manipulation, leave. Do not try to explain anything to the narcissist, you will only be ripped to shreds. Get out and go no contact.

Cold hearted – The narcissist is unfeeling toward you. Be very clear about that. The narcissist lacks empathy and lacks love toward you. If he has told you he loves you, you need to know that it's not true. It's an illusion. It's a lie. It's a con. It's a manipulation. It's a game. His heart is black and empty.

Communication – The point of conversation with a narcissist is about his needs, his wants, his desires, his expectations. Listen closely as the narcissist uses many "I" statements as well as the other first-person pronouns (me, mine). The narcissist needs to be the center of the conversation, either while engaged in it, or the topic of it. The narcissist does not communicate well. He will say he "did not hear" a piece of what his conversation partner said. Be clear, it's not that he "did not hear" the person speaking. The true reason is that he was not listening. Instead of owning what was said during communication, he will avoid it, ignore it, evade, and lie, and so on. When the narcissist wants something that the narcissist is not getting, the narcissist will badger, intimidate, spin question, deflect, make fun of, and degrade the other person.

■ Again, listen closely to the narcissist. He will try to be evasive. If you pay attention, you can hear him zigzag around a topic to confuse you and get you off track.

■ Be certain of this, there are ulterior motives whenever you are talking with a narcissist. The only thing the narcissist wants is what is good for the narcissist's agenda—whatever it may be.

■ The narcissist purposefully miscommunicates with you in order to confuse you. Your head will spin.

■ The narcissist will avoid conversation and communication when he is wrong. He will become silent. He will cease the conversation, saying something like he has to leave. He will even run away from a conversation during the middle of a conversation. Let him leave, or hang up on you because he is behaving like a child. (He loves to hang up on you to teach you a lesson and to show you that you are worthless to him. The only thing he is showing you is that he has lost control of himself and does not know how to communicate.) You are a grown woman who should be with a grown man.

Comparison – It is not acceptable for the person you are with to compare you to others, at all, ever. You are an awesome, unique, special person who stands in comparison to no one.

Competitive – The narcissist is in some sort of twisted competition with most everyone. The win/lose mentality of the narcissist shows in almost all aspects of his life either overtly or covertly. The narcissist does anything to win: lie, cheat, steal, destroy, manipulate, degrade, and bully. The narcissist wants you to lose in some sort of way (even when you win) to inflate their own pathetic being. The narcissist believes he is the best at everything: biking, their job, running, sports, the best shows, the best board game player, the best card player. The narcissist might likely seem to be the best as well as the narcissist is very strategic. This strategic mind that you once admired will be used against you to manipulate you, control you, and ultimately destroy you.

Complex relationship – He is not as dynamic or complex as he likes to believe he is. He is mean, strategic, a liar, and a manipulator. His development is nonexistent or is stunted. He is a fake man-child.

Complains – The narcissist will passively aggressive complain, or will outfight complain about people, subjects, events, money, issues. You name it. Of course, we all complain from time to time. The narcissist looks for reasons to complain. The narcissist then feels his complaint is so egregious and so damning (even if minor) that if you do not agree and/or do something about it, you are worthless and the enemy. The complaint the narcissist looked for, found, and spouted becomes secondary and you now become the primary problem.

Conceited – Whether it is overt and right out there, or it is covert and the narcissist has the flying monkeys do his dirty work for him, the narcissist has an over-inflated sense of self and is self-centered. Again, this can be overt or covert. Watch out for the covert narcissist. He is a sneaky snake.

Conclusions – The narcissist will jump to conclusions about you. The narcissist will make up conclusions about your actions, the things you are doing, places you are going, and so on. The narcissist will even make up his own conclusions about your thoughts. If you try to defend or "explain yourself" (which is the position the narcissist likes to place you in to further his arguments and to find something to prove or justify his crazymaking), you will only end up frustrating yourself; and you will be fueling his fire. Don't be tricked. Don't explain yourself to him because it's a trap! It's a trap you cannot escape from because it will only go around and around and around. Don't engage in feeding the monster.

Condescending – The narcissist will use condescending language and a condescending tone with you to make you feel inferior. The narcissist is so internally weak and pathetic he is unable to communicate in a rational, adult manner without making someone else feel bad. That's his immature developmental level. You are an adult, working off of adult communication. The narcissist is not working off the same developmental level. It's an illusion when he does.

Conditioning – The narcissist will program you to fit his agenda. The narcissist will use your weakness and wounds to manipulate you and condition you. The narcissist will condition you to desire him, worry if he's going to call or not/show up or not. The narcissist will condition you to jump and to be available when the narcissist wants you. The narcissist will condition you to keep secrets. The narcissist will condition you to lose your self-worth. The narcissist will condition you to want him, desire him, to seek approval from him, and to please him (or else there will be consequences). This will occur even after you have been hurt by the narcissist, and you know that this person is a jerk or toxic. You will still have these strong emotional ties to the narcissist. The narcissist has implanted them in you. You will be confused why the narcissist can so easily leave you (after you've endured his crazymaking and you tried so hard to prove how "good" or "beneficial" you are to be with someone else. That is because you are worthless to the narcissist. You are nothing to the narcissist. The narcissist never loved you. The narcissist used you. This is conditioning. When the narcissist circles back, or harasses you after you have left, do not, under any circumstances, engage with the narcissist. Seek help in learning how to break the abuse cycle and to build a healthy self-esteem.

Confidence – The narcissist will become intimate with you very quickly. During this intimate, personal time, you will open up and share, or confide, in this amazing person you think is the love of your life. The narcissist will use these weaknesses you lovingly shared during the private vulnerable time you two spent together to manipulate, exploit, hurt, even blackmail you. (By the way, anyone who does this is not the love of your life. Anyone who does this is not your friend. Anyone who does this is unkind and toxic.)

Confides – The narcissist gets you to tell him your secrets. He will share some stories from his childhood, stories of his glory days, with some tales of woe thrown in there . . . but evasive as well. Most certainly the narcissist will "need" you for something, something that requires you to become emotionally involved. Perhaps he thinks he has cancer or a brain tumor. He will have you go along with him to the doctor's office for "moral support." (Do you feel honored he "neeeeeeds youuuuuu?" Don't. It's a trick. He does this with everyone.)

Confiding – Do not tell your secrets to in someone you barely know regardless how much love bombing there is, or how much you think you are soulmates. (You are not soulmates.) Do not give a person, who you've known less than a year, all your secrets (and passwords and credit cards). Be selective. If after a year you have had smooth sailing and are in a healthy relationship, then proceed. Anyone who wants to know everything there is to know about you so fast is up to something and has an agenda. Usually, no good can come from the super-fast relationship. It's a red flag warning!

Conning – The narcissist uses events, illnesses, deaths, work, emergencies, children, the weather, vacations, cars, money, clothing, gifts, and even pets to engage and trick the target.

Conscience – The narcissist does not have consistent values, ethics, or conscience. You are meaningless to the narcissist, so are your feelings and emotions. The narcissist will hurt you emotionally, mentally, and physically and not think twice about it.

Consequences – The narcissist does not seem to suffer repercussions for his actions. This is because he has no concern or care about how things affect others and is not bothered by other issues that he has caused. He moves on to the next thing with rapid speed. He has no connection. If you bring something up that he did to you, you will be blamed for causing drama and "not letting it go." The "it" can be anything from physical violence to rude behavior on his part. He does not care about you so why should the narcissist bother talking about it.

Constructive criticism – There is no such thing as constructive helpful critique where the narcissist is concerned. Anything short of agreeing with the narcissist is considered an attack by the narcissist.

Contempt – The narcissist feels disgust for you, and for most others. If you are filling a need for him, you're good to go (for a while anyway); but he still doesn't truly care about or for you. (Make no mistake about that.) If you don't fit his agenda, you are not necessary. You are worthless to him. He will chip away at your self-worth so you feel contempt. (He's a real peach; isn't he?)

Context – Have you been accused of taking the statements or words used by the narcissist "out of context?" Have you been accused of "misunderstanding" something that you are very clear in knowing? Guess what. The narcissist is pulling an evasive, gaslighting, manipulative tactic on you.

Contradictory – The narcissist will change his opinions, personal "beliefs," rules, likes, dislikes, on a whim, if it suit's his needs and his agenda. This change may contradict things the narcissist has said in the past and even says currently. There's no rhyme or reason to the scattered, unintelligible, spiny "logic" of the narcissist. This spiny logic will ultimately make you feel as though you are spinning on an out of control carousel in a twisted madhouse. The contradictions are meant to throw you off balance and to gain control over you.

Control – The narcissist is all about having power over you (by taking your power away from you). The narcissist makes you believe that he is concerned for you. Wants to know your comings and goings to make sure you are safe. Or, the abuser may want to take over tasks to "help" you. Of course, the abuser will find errors with all that he helps you, therefore, beginning the chipping away at your self-worth. The reality is, the narcissist does not feel as though he is in control and is afraid he will be discovered as a fraud (which the narcissist is). Because he lacks self-control, he instead turns his need for control of the people around him. A narcissist appears to be in absolute control always and takes great pride in boasting this. He feels as though he is hyper-alert to protect himself and others against danger and violence. He has a need to be the hero. He must be acknowledged for giving assistance, helping, and doing chores, as well as protecting you or others in a public place. The narcissist believes that everyone else is not paying attention and he will be the hero should something go amiss. These are thoughts of grandeur. Control is also a lack of empathy. You are not a priority. The narcissist is looking at you wondering what the approach he will use to manipulate you and control you. When you leave, you need help getting through recovery.

■ 2. Narcissistic control over has created chaos in your very active mind. You want calm, inner peace, and balance restored in your life. Your over-active monkey mind will seek the chaos because chaos is what it knows. The chaos is like a drug addiction. A drug addict does not want the drugs, knows the drugs are counterproductive, and makes the resolve not to take them anymore; but, he craves the drugs and falls into the cycle of wanting them again. It is a cycle that can only be stopped with the help of professionals. This is exactly how a toxic relationship, including a narcissistic relationship, is. YOU MUST GET HELP through the recovery.

Convincing – The narcissist wooed you, love-bombed you, and now has your heart. The love bombing seems real. The narcissist will next begin a process of convincing you how awful you are, how you don't measure up, how you are overly dramatic, how you are needy, how you are crazy, how you are worthless. Why does he do this? It is his insecurities. It is a projection of how he feels. To feel better about himself, the narcissist must tear you (and others) down. He gets a misguided feeling of superiority for being "right" and for tearing down, or belittling, or destroying another person. Everything the narcissist is saying to you is an example of his behavior. He is projecting onto you. The lies he tells others about you to malign you sound plausible. It has nothing to do with you—it's all him. His rage or disgust is pointed toward you, but it is his childish insecurity showing through. He is toxic and will never change. Regardless if the person is a narcissist or not, if someone is treating you as if you don't measure up, turn and run and go no contact. There is no reason whatsoever you need this toxic person in your life. Don't try to prove the truth to him or to anyone. By trying to prove the truth, you are still under the control of the narcissist. Anyone who has faith in you will nurture you. Anyone who feeds off drama will be pulled into the web. Let them be. Let them walk. You begin your new, drama-free life this minute!

Convoluted – The narcissist will create lies and stories simply to avoid telling you the truth. Regardless if what you are asking is simple, the narcissist believes you are being suspicious and will lie to "throw you off the track." This is done to distract and confuse you, and to ultimately hurt your feelings by making you seem inferior or conniving in some sort of way. He believes he is justified in lying to you.

Counterproductive – The narcissist is a threat to your happiness and emotional well-being. The narcissist is counterproductive to your goal attainment. The narcissist is counterproductive in the workplace. The narcissist's extreme low self-esteem and self-loathing is set on destruct. He has an internal drive to be destructive to others while at the same time giving the illusion of "saving the day," "being the most intelligent one," or "the only one who can do this task/job/position/program." (Sometimes the narcissist will create problems in order to be the one to solve them.)

Courage – Once you lovingly share your weaknesses, your self-worth and confidence will be taken from you and squashed using your very own weaknesses that you lovingly shared/confided in this person you thought was your soulmate. (He isn't.)

Covert – The narcissist will behave in underhanded, subtly, sneaky, passive-aggressive ways. Not all the narcissist's tricks are blatant, out there, in your face. The narcissist is a manipulator. The narcissist will use whatever the narcissist needs to do to break your spirit to put you under the narcissist's control.

Covert narcissist (also known as introverted narcissist, vulnerable narcissist, hypersensitive narcissist, closet narcissist) – From the research I've done and the experience I have had with someone who is typical example of the covert narcissist, the covert narcissist is no fool and is a strategic sneaky snake who acts like a victim all the time. The covert narcissist is quiet, subdued, polite, and if need be he will play the role of needy and pathetic. The covert narcissist will even trick you into apologizing to him for his bad behavior and manipulations of situations. The covert narcissist is a clever predator, maybe even more so than the obvious overt narcissist. Beware of this sneaky snake. As you become more and more intertwined with him, he will wreak havoc and chaos in an almost gentle, elegant, and passive manner. Make no mistake about it: the quiet covert narcissist has an agenda to "fit in" and take you down and make you suffer. He wants to control and dominate you, just as the overt narcissist does, but has a different approach. The relationship will be unbalanced, unhealthy, and will leave you lonely and sad. His needs, wants, and desires are primary. He does not love you. He has never loved you. He will never love you. You are not his soulmate.

Coward – The narcissist is a brutal coward. Narcissists have low self-esteem. To feel better about himself, he plays mental and emotional games with other's feelings, compassion, and life. The narcissist is a coward because he is not self-reflective. He is too afraid to see who he really is because it is ugly. He hides behind a fake persona that he has copied from someone who is truly worthy. The narcissist is not the attentive person you think he is. It's an illusion.

Crazy – The narcissist will make you feel worthless, as though you're crazy. You will lose your sense of self. You will lose your self-confidence. This is a manipulation called gaslighting. You need to leave the unbalanced relationship immediately. You need to seek help from an expert in recovering your self-esteem and identity.

Crazy train – It strikes me as humorous that one of my former husband's most favorite songs was "Crazy Train." I would often say, "I feel like I'm on a crazy train." Or, "I want off the crazy train." I wanted off the crazy train so much so I tried to end my life. The narcissist will tell you who he is right out in the open. He will tell you he is "broken" or "damaged." He does this in a manner so that you feel compassion and empathy for him. You need to listen and not write it off as, "He just needs love," or "He's just joking," because he is not joking. He is damaged and he wants to hurt you and bring you down to his hell lifestyle. (On a side note: while his song was "Crazy Train," my favorite song was "Always" and "Crazy for You." He saw me, the empath and the romantic, coming a mile away.)

Crazymaking – Feel in a tizzy? The narcissist is creating havoc wherever he goes with his crazymaking ways. The narcissist does this because the narcissist really has no sense of self. The narcissist is living in an illusion based reality of delusion depending on others to make him feel whole . . . to make him "feel" something. This is impossible. When you realize what is going on, don't try to fix the narcissist. The narcissist cannot be fixed, nor do you have the training to attempt this. You need to seek help in regaining your life, your true self, and to learn how to not allow a narcissist back in your life.

■ The narcissist will create havoc and will navigate you to the middle of it. Either you will be to blame for the crazymaking the narcissist has caused. Or you have not fully supported the crazymaking of the narcissist. Either way, you are in a no-win situation. You need to find a more balanced, equally loving, and nurturing relationship. This one isn't is.

Crisis – The narcissist seems to love a disaster and an emergency. His internal state seems to always be in flux, which seems like an angry crisis. He, himself, has many crises. His problems may be with work, you, medical, and so on. He has crises so he can garner sympathy from people. He wants to see who will be loyal to him, who "cares" about him (although the care is not reciprocated), and how many people he can take advantage of. He will have an agenda—which could be monetary, or emotional. The narcissist also seems to relish in other's true crises. He wants to be the one to "save the day." When he "saves the day" he will receive praise. The narcissist loves being the center of attention and receiving praise (even covert narcissists enjoy this).

Criticize – The narcissist will disapprove and will find fault with you overtly and covertly. This may be done disguised as a "helpful" points so that you are able to "improve" for him. He will outwardly insult you in an immature way as well. You will feel put down and worthless. You will begin to question yourself. You should never feel this way with anyone—certainly not with someone with whom you are in a relationship. The first time this happens, turn and run and go no contact from the narcissist. No one should ever purposefully and cruelly find fault with you.

Critiques – The narcissist will "evaluate" and "assess" you by comparing you to someone else. This is cruel—which is the narcissist's intent to bring you under the narcissist's control. (Personally, I was given a daily evaluation on four points: how clean the house was, if I was showered and looked nice for him, if I had made lunch, dinner, and snacks for the day, and a sexual evaluation. For these tasks, I was given up to $20 a week for my allowance. Every year I received a formal evaluation and discussion where I had had strengths and areas where I needed to improve. CONTROL for him. I had given him my power.) Run, girls. If someone is mean to you, "for your own good," get out of there as fast as you can!

Cruel – The narcissist is cruel. The cruelty can come in the forms of emotional abuse, physical abuse, mental abuse, sexual abuse, financial abuse, controlling abuse. Generally, narcissistic abuse pulls from all types of abuse. The narcissist IS cruel towards anything that takes time and/or attention away from him. This includes his own children and pets. If it takes attention away from the narcissist, the narcissist will be cruel toward it. My former spouse gave away my beloved westies to a coworker; then tried to have them killed. Heartless. This is typical for the toxic, self-centered person. The pet or the child needs attention for the bathroom, clean up for sickness, and shedding. The abuser will have unrealistic expectations for the children and pets. If his unrealistic expectations are part of his unrealistic image management.

Cursing – Studies show that narcissists tend to use offensive or derogatory words, swear words, sexual innuendo, sexual language more so than other people. (He might frustrate, hurt, even anger you so much so you slip into depression and begin to use swear words. This is a red flag. Run!)

Cycles – Feels threatened (the other person is not under his control) -> uses abuse tactics to regain control -> becomes the victim -> feels empowered. To control you, the narcissist will use a hot/cold cycle where he is paying attention to you and then nothing, withdrawing affection and attention. This is also called breadcrumbing. He will throw you a bone to pull you back into his lady stable of narcissistic supply.

D

Dangerous – A narcissist, a person with narcissistic traits, a person with narcissistic features, who is toxic, or is simply a jerk is dangerous to your emotional well-being. This type of person is filled with jealousy and insecurity. This type of person has an agenda. This type of person wants to make you feel inferior. This dangerous person wants to destroy you so that he can feel superior.

Death – The narcissist always has some sort of ailment or disease which requires extensive medical research because the doctors cannot find anything wrong with him. Nothing at all. The narcissist is so fixated on these mysterious diseases because he is probably afraid of death and his afterlife consequence: an eternity in hell.

Deception – A narcissist is a blame-shifter, a liar, and a manipulator. The narcissist wants to deceive you. The narcissist wants to deceive everyone. The narcissist thinks you're stupid and that the narcissist has gotten away with something through the lies and manipulation he has used. You were either bamboozled by this and are in a state of bafflement/confusion/or blindsiding. This is meant to chip away at your self-worth and self-esteem and to create self-questioning of yourself. The reason the narcissist is doing this is that it is filling a need in his pathetic, low self-esteem life. If someone makes you feel bamboozled or confused, regardless if he is a narcissist or not, go no contact as this is a toxic person you do not want or need in your life.

Decision making – The abusive partner wants you to be dependent upon him. The toxic person will systematically tear you down so that simple decisions become very difficult. The abuser is chipping away at your self-confidence and self-worth. Your decision-making skills will begin to deteriorate. You will question everything. The abusive partner wants you deferring to him.

Decline – When you decline an offer, an invitation, or gift from the narcissist, if you are in the love bombing stage, the narcissist will push your boundaries by putting you in the position to defend your reasoning why you are declining. Should you decline an offer, you will be punished by the narcissist.

Defective – The narcissist will treat you as if there is something wrong with you when he's disgusted with Heaven knows what, or wants a narcissistic fix, or simply wants to make you feel inferior. YOU are not defective! If anyone makes you feel bad about your being you, then leave this person so you can find someone who will appreciate you for you. You want to be with someone who LIKES you.

Defend – The narcissist will justify and support his lies, games, and manipulations till the end. The narcissist's goal is to make you bend into submission (and then using the silent treatment to punish you and put you in your place).

■ The narcissist uses other people, aka "the flying monkeys," to defend him. He's a coward and will not display who he is with emotionally and mentally healthy people for fear of being found out. Instead, the narcissist uses the flying monkeys who appear to be healthy to do the narcissist's dirty work for him. They are just as unhealthy as the narcissist. They may be narcissists as well. (They usually are.)

Defending yourself – With the various humiliation, triangulation, lies, manipulations, fantasy stories made up by the narcissist, you will feel compelled to defend yourself, your character (that he's likely attacked), and your name. Don't engage in the set of immature events that the narcissist has started defaming or slandering about you. If it is actionable, contact an attorney. Otherwise, let the petty, immature narcissist and his flying monkeys' gossip about you, and spread lies about you because the narcissist's lies will eventually present themselves and the narcissist will hang himself. He might say you are an excessive spender, when in fact he empties the bank account to 19 cents because he has secret bank accounts. The proof will reveal itself. Do not bother spending the energy on the narcissist's immature behaviors. Generally, soon after the narcissist has a new person in his life, you are forgotten as he begins his cycle of control and domination with someone else. Take back YOUR POWER and YOUR CONTROL by not engaging with the lies. That's what the narcissist wants you to do. That is the narcissist's strategy. Again, if it's actionable, and you can prove it, hire an attorney.

Defensive – The narcissist will put you on the defense in almost every situation (regardless of the importance of the situation). This is done by the narcissist's belittling which causes you to self-question, second guess, and devalue yourself. You will walk on eggshells and will feel as though you are always defending your actions.

■ The narcissist is uber defensive if you question him. Any question, regardless of how innocent, will be treated as an invasion.

Defer – The narcissist will avoid decision making, creating plans with you, and commitments you are interested in upholding. The narcissist defers so long that the choices will become limited to nothing favorable . . . and the narcissist may not even want to do them. This happens because the narcissist has no sense of self, so the narcissist is unable to decide. Should you take the reins, you will be criticized. The narcissist wants what the narcissist wants and even the narcissist doesn't even know what that is but will complain about whatever outcome occurs. (Make sense? No, it doesn't. Welcome to a relationship with a narcissist.)

Defiling – The narcissist will tear you apart to other people while with you and when you are no longer together. The narcissist is not loyal. The narcissist does not care to protect your image or your reputation. The narcissist wants to destroy it to make the narcissist feel better and more superior to you. This is a toxic human being.

Deflated – The narcissist feels deflated. The only way to make the narcissist feel better about himself is to tear another person down and make the target feel deflated and therefore creating another victim. If you are feeling deflated in a relationship, you need to go no contact and get help in healing.

Deflect – The narcissist is unable to acknowledge and own his actions. The narcissist will blame shift or deflect his actions onto someone else. Most often that person is you. The narcissist can take any point you want to talk about and will turn it around, dilute it, and will make you a bad guy, leaving you to feel baffled, hurt, and sad. It will never be safe for the target, you, to bring up any topic that is bothering you, regardless of significance or importance. The narcissist does not care about you, or your puny issues and will make you pay for bringing it to his attention. It will not end well. It ever does. (See also "Motive questions.)

Demanding – The narcissist is insistent in having most everything "his way" for his comfort, needs, and desires regardless of others' needs. The narcissist is often unreasonably demanding at that. It is difficult, nearly impossible, to truly always please the narcissist. The narcissist will breadcrumb you by praising you for something; but, then will criticize you for not meeting the narcissist's needs shortly thereafter . . . or before to make you compliant and work harder for the narcissist. The narcissist uses demands to create anxiety and confusion along with the loss of self-worth in the target.

Demean – Narcissists idealize you, love bomb you and then begin to take away your dignity to make himself feel better. They go from loving and adoring you to making you feel stupid and inferior. The narcissist will make you feel/believe that you have so many problems when you try to talk to him about something that bothers you. The narcissist demeans your feelings.

Demoralize – The narcissist wants you to give away your power, and wants you to develop low self-esteem, and even lose your confidence. Either obviously or subtly, the narcissist will berate and belittle you. The narcissist is full of tricks, tactics, and manipulations to strip you of who you are. Should you begin to feel "less than" or in a state of flux, notice this as a red flag and get help for yourself to improve your self-esteem. You deserve better; and better is out there waiting for you.

Denial – The narcissist will make you question yourself and your judgment. You may find yourself in denial of the truth and of reality. You will have gut feelings that you explain away. Don't explain away things. Instead, honor your instincts. Your instincts are in place to protect you from danger. The narcissist is just that: danger, danger, danger.

Derailing – The narcissist will purposefully lead you in a direction you don't want to go. This is the big switcheroo and it happens so quickly. The narcissist is a master at switching things like derailing conversations—especially if you are making valid points or suggestions. If you are in a conversation and have been derailed, you keep the focus. You bring the focus back. (That will annoy, even infuriate the narcissist.) The narcissist will derail your plans. The narcissist will derail your life so get out as soon as you notice red flags. Honor your instincts.

Despair – You will likely end up feeling like you are in desperation of hopelessness and demoralized when you are with the narcissist (and even during the no contact). Seek help from friends, family, and specialists to get help. I promise you, there is light at the other end of the tunnel. I was in despair, very weak, one day during recovery. I sent a text to my cousin. She showed up bearing white cake with white icing and stayed with me while I cried, laughed, cried, talked, cried, stared, pondered, worried, wondered and so on. She stayed with me nonjudgmentally until after my father came home. She doesn't know it, but she saved my life that afternoon. I am forever grateful to her.

Desperate – Did you behave as a hopeless woman in despair before the narcissist was in your life? You probably didn't. The narcissist manipulated you into this state. To break free from this feeling, you need to regain your self-worth. Make an appointment with a specialist to help you. In the meantime, dump this creep, call your friends and go out. Have some guilt-free fun!

Destroyer of property – The narcissist does not respect your personal boundaries. The narcissist does not respect your property. The narcissist may even be so arrogant to believe that your things belong to him. The narcissist would rather destroy your things than just walk away.

Destroyer of self – The narcissist is intent on attacking your sense of self and self-confidence. The narcissist does this by getting into your mind and corrupting your thoughts. The narcissist plays mind games with you planting seeds of doubt and worry at every instance the narcissist can.

Detach – You must disengage, disconnect, and remove yourself from the narcissist to heal. This is only achieved by going no contact from the abuser. The narcissist is mentally and emotionally detached from you (and most people). The narcissist does not deserve you, your heart, your emotions, love. The narcissist doesn't know what to do with them anyway; and, will never give the same back to you in return. Go no contact from him. Block him on your phone, your social media, and change all passwords immediately.

Detached – The narcissist is disconnected and separated from you emotionally and mentally. The narcissist does not love you, has never loved you. (He probably even told you that. Listen to this, it's true!). The narcissist will never love you in the future. The only person the narcissist has any emotion for is for himself. Generally, that emotion isn't even love—it is self-loathing. The narcissist does not like love and probably has a hit out on Cupid.

Devaluing – The narcissist enjoys finding reasons to belittle you, shame you, and make fun of you. The narcissist has no allegiance to you. The narcissist does not value you, what you've done for the narcissist, how you've helped the narcissist, the sacrifices you've made for the narcissist, or how you are loyal to the narcissist. The narcissist will treat you as a pathetic, dramatic person. My advice is to go no contact. Call someone to get help in healing from narcissistic abuse.

Developmental stages – Erik Erikson developed eight stages of development. At each stage, a person can experience a crisis in which the development either progresses or is stunted. The narcissist does not seem to have moved through the stages of development. This is not your problem. You are not trained to help or fix him. Usually, the narcissist does not want fixed or "helped" (he will say he does, but it is a manipulation to string you along). Only a trained specialist should work with a suspected narcissist.

Dignity – The narcissist wants to take your self-worth and dignity away from you. Go no contact.

Dilutes – The narcissist will divert attention from an issue if an issue is against him, and from the impact his behavior has caused. His behavior. The narcissist will change the subject altogether instead of truly and fully taking responsibility or ownership. The narcissist will deflect and will blame others. The narcissist will even create another level of façade of how he is wonderful and benevolent instead of the monster, abuser, cheater, and creep he is. This façade will be interjected with "when I was a child . . ." Yes, the narcissist loves to throw in his own real/ contrived trauma from childhood. The thing is, we have all endured trauma as children, but we don't behave in the manner the narcissist does. The narcissist even expects to ride the trauma train for pity from empaths for the rest of his life. Grow up, narcissist. Oh wait, that's one thing you CAN'T do. Regardless of the narcissist's place in society, the church, the job, or in the family, the narcissist is stuck at a lower emotional developmental level. The narcissist is forever immature.

Diminished – You were once vibrant. Now you feel unsure of yourself. You feel small. The narcissist has used manipulations on you to diminish your value. Leave this toxic relationship now. It will only get worse. You need to seek help to become empowered.

Disagree – Disagreeing with a narcissist is an opportunity for the narcissist to unleash his wrath on you. It will be so verbally brutal (and possibly physically brutal) that you will end up feeling so ashamed for being alive. The narcissist enjoys this type of interaction. He will also blame you for causing drama . . . for having an opinion.

Disappearing act – The narcissist will complain you are too needy and that the narcissist is spending all his time with you. The narcissist will let you know how very little he wants to spend time with you. He will make you feel like a drag. The manipulation the narcissist is likely undertaking is that the narcissist is cheating on you. When you discover this, or you ask the narcissist about this, the narcissist will disappear from your life as a punishment. This will cause you anxiety, and make you feel bad about yourself.

Disappointed – Because the narcissist is unable to commit to ideas, events, people, when plans fall through (because of the narcissist's own issues), the narcissist will present himself as disappointed and displeased. When it's pointed out that he did not want to do it, or did not offer a commitment for the activity, he will say he did and that you weren't listening to him. This is a lie. The narcissist is a victim of his own lack of commitment resulting in disappointment. You can verify and confirm as much as you want, when the time comes around that it is event time and you're not there, the narcissist will express his victim mentality of disappointment because he "thought we were going." That's not true. Disappointment will turn into shaming you and or anger toward you. When you realize this game, you need to know there are many, many, many more manipulations being run on you. Leave this toxic relationship. It is not going to get better, even if you "talk" it over. (It will only get worse.)

Disarm – To disarm something or someone means to take away the power or the fuse. The narcissist uses a disarming tactic of blindsiding you with confusion to throw you off, confuse you, and to deteriorate your self-confidence, self-worth, and to make you question yourself. The narcissist's absolute intent is to take away your power, self-worth, self-confidence, intelligence. You do not need to be disarmed.

Discard – The abuser wants to create a sense of dependency of him in you by instilling anxiety and worry. He will go missing in action and will discard you without notice. This will create confusion for you. He will discard you, break up with you, or push you aside easily. Do not chase after a man who will discard you for any reason. It is not nice. It is not a balanced relationship. It is certainly not love.

Discredit – The narcissist will dispute you by attacking your character. You could be the chaste and pure Sister Angelina and the narcissist will attack your character in an attempt to dishonor you, make you feel stupid, or slam your reputation.

Disempower – You wanted to love. You were left with anxiety, hopelessness, and a very disempowering state of being. This is exactly what the narcissist wanted. You need to go no contact from him. You need to seek help from a professional because you are more than enough! You are powerful! You are awesome! It is still inside of you. Let it out and let it shine!

Disengage – You need to remove yourself from the toxic person and toxic situations. You need to go no contact from the abusive person in your life. Do not engage!

Disengaged – At first, the narcissist wants to spend all his time with you. The narcissist showers you with attention and affection. Once you have fallen in love (and rather fast at that), the narcissist will pull away, disengage, fall off the side of the earth. Should you ask what is going on, or if you did something (the narcissist wants you to think that of yourself), the narcissist will say you are too needy. The narcissist is disengaged from you because the narcissist was never truly invested in you in the first place. It was an illusion—a game. The narcissist will tell you he never loved you. You were "just there." It hurts. It's painful. Remember this pain because the narcissist will circle back for another go at your emotions. Don't fall for this trick. Go no contact. You are not needy—the narcissist made you that way. You take your life and your emotions back. Seek help in recovering from narcissistic emotional abuse.

Dishonest – A narcissist will boast how honest the narcissist is. That would be fake news. The narcissist doesn't know how to be honest. The narcissist isn't even honest with himself to let alone anyone else. The narcissist's existence is based on lies he tells himself and lies he tells others.

Dismissive – The narcissist is not interested in your likes, dislikes, interests, work, career, charities, and volunteerism. He could care less about you and them. Being dismissive is how he will show you, from his point of view, that you are worthless. Unless he is in a highlighted position, you can forget about participation and support. He may even complain that you are spending too much time working, volunteering, being charitable, and so on. He will say you are spending too much time away from him. He will use this as his excuse to cheat, punish you, give you the silent treatment, and so on. It's your fault he strayed. (Um, no it isn't, but that is the mind of the immature toxic abuser.) After he complains and you pull back on your activities, then he will pull back on you. It's his strategic game. He got want he wanted: you complying with his demands. It was a game . . . and he won. Now he will likely go missing in action.

Dispassionate – The narcissist, or toxic individual, will say he is beyond passion because he is extremely logical and overly rational. He sits back and "takes it all in." Riiiiight. Surrrre. He lacks passion. He wears an emotional mask because he doesn't really know who he is. He needs to get over himself. And you need to remove yourself from this creep.

Disrespectful – The narcissist sees you, and most everyone else, as objects. The narcissist has no respect for you. The narcissist will disrespect you in private; and if the narcissist is arrogant, will disrespect you in public as well. This type of public humiliation is one of the narcissist's ways to see how far he can go with you, and with the audience. If the audience is accepting of it, the narcissist may find a flying monkey or two. Once you are disrespected (and embarrassed), don't give the toxic person a second chance to do it again. It's not a joke—being mean and rude is never a joke. It is an indicator of who the narcissist really is.

Dissatisfied – After the love bombing and the constant praise of you and everything about you, you will find that he is less and less satisfied with you and everything else in his life . . . as well as yours (to the narcissist, you are, after all, a reflection of him). You are now beginning to see the true person behind the narcissist mask he was wearing to hide who he really is: a miserable, extremely low self-esteem, self-hating human being. (Nothing you can do will improve his situation or outlook.)

Distant – After the narcissist has you in his clutches, he will begin to distance himself from you. Then will reappear . . . and will become distant again. This twisted dance continues for some time. This is conditioning you to appear to become "needy" for the narcissist individual. You may even feel like you are losing control and in fact are becoming the needy person. That's because your defenses are down and you are allowing a toxic person to slowly assume control of you and your emotions. Take them back by going no contact with the narcissist. You do not need the narcissist regardless of what he's done in the past for you. That was a manipulation to make you fall for him. The good days are gone. The narcissist is "breadcrumbing" you. Go no contact. Find someone who is awesome who will elevate you instead of being distant from you.

■ You could be in the same room with the narcissist and feel a million miles away from him. That's because the narcissist is aloof and the narcissist's natural energy is void. If you are feeling distant, notice the red flag. It's not you. It's the narcissist.

Divergent – The narcissist will add unnecessary information to a decision-making process to smoke screen you and to add confusion. The sneaky narcissist does not want to make a commitment to an activity, an ideal, or a person. You will feel like you are participating in a verbal back and forth Ping-Pong match. This is used so the narcissist avoids making any real commitment to something so the narcissist can be righteously disappointed, upset, or angry because the narcissist will say he wanted to do the thing he avoided committing to in the first place. It's a game so the narcissist can be a wounded victim of not getting his way . . . once again. The narcissist is always disappointed.

Divide and conquer – The narcissist attempts to control everything about you (including your finances, resources personal development, interests, appearance, and hobbies), and to destroy your self-worth. The narcissist will divide you from your support. The narcissist will belittle the people you love or admire to make you feel ashamed. The narcissist will say unkind things about you to them and will say unkind things about them to you. The narcissist will put you in situations where you will be harassed, treated unkindly, or engaged in conversations that are hostile. Divide and conquer is also part of the triangulation tactic.

Divorce – The narcissist makes promises during pre-attorney discussions. The narcissist says he will "give you" what is fair. The narcissist says he will pay for the divorce. Lies. The narcissist is a liar. The narcissist believes you deserve nothing, zero, zip. The narcissist has lied the entire time you've been married. Do not start thinking the narcissist is suddenly going to be a standup guy now. No way. The narcissist is intent on destroying you. The narcissist will attempt to paint you as greedy, spoiled, and overly pampered. (You lived with a narcissist. You are anything but overly pampered.) The narcissist will not waiver on alimony, equitable distribution, support. Instead, the narcissist will drag it out until you succumb to what he wants. If you have a protection of abuse against him (or have them against each other), you must make sure you have the children, and the pets. The narcissist will use other people, and your pets to antagonize you, hurt you, and destroy you. Remember the narcissist has no empathy for anything. The narcissist does not care about animals and will allow them to suffer.

Documentation – The narcissist will threaten, harass, invade your privacy, stalk you, hack you, and do things you cannot even imagine. You must document even the most innocuous, seemingly innocent, incidents that give you a warning in your mind. You must document it because the abuse will add up. You need to alert the police, your attorney, counselor, therapist, family doctor, and anyone who is required to keep documentation on you. You may need this information in court. You may need this information to save your life.

Dominant dog – Narcissists are cowards and are pathetic. He lives his life in victim mentality, albeit sometimes aggressively with his victim mentality of blaming others. The covert narcissist is no exception. He is driven to be the center of the universe as well. Narcissists attempt to overcompensate their inferior feeling by copying traits of a dog on the loose who does not understand cooperation. This is a developmentally immature person. You deserve better than immature dominant dog man-child. Surround yourself with empowering, wonderful, compassionate friends and family when you leave this person. You will need their support. The narcissist will likely act up and bombard you with irrational communication when you do not react to his punishments and silent treatments.

Domineering – The narcissist wants to dominate and be domineering over you and most interactions with others in some way. This is done so the narcissist can exploit you and/or those in the group. If it is covertly, then the pity or victim factor is likely to be the dominating piece. The narcissist, covertly, tells victim tales. When the covert narcissist has side pieces, the narcissist is the victim in his stories from his main partner. The narcissist gains pity from the lies he tells.

Double standard – Standards and expectations by narcissists are all over the board and change constantly. It's confusing and meant to be so. The narcissist has no idea what is "right" for his circumstance, so the standard changes constantly. It's as if you are a bowling ball a match of bowling. You think you know which pins to tumble to get spared. The narcissist will pick up the pins just as the ball is coming his way. You will never win. You will never get a spare . . . nor will you be spared the wrath of the narcissist. The narcissist can do anything he wants; you cannot. The narcissist can talk to anyone he wants; you cannot. The narcissist can laugh at anything he wants; you cannot.

Doubting reality – The narcissist will tell you lies, report things to you that were allegedly said about you, and will twist the truth. The narcissist is making you question yourself and your sense of reality. When you notice that you are questioning yourself or feel confused often, get out of this twisted, toxic relationship.

Dr. Jekyll/Mr. Hyde – The narcissist will be giving you affection, telling you nice things one moment, then suddenly is giving you the silent treatment and will refuse to look at you or acknowledge your presence. Or you are snuggling on the couch, and bam, switch flipped and he is screaming at you. You might be all set to celebrate an achievement, but the narcissist attacks you verbally and will not stop. Nothing you can say or do can make it better. Or the reverse will happen: the narcissist calls you screaming about nonsense and will hang up on you (a favorite activity of his); then will call back lovey-dovey (without an apology) ready to decorate the holiday tree and be a couple again.

Drag you down – Making you feel worthless, like the shell of a person, is exactly what the narcissist's purpose and mission are. The narcissist is emotionally low-level, a bottom feeder. He wants to bring you and your positive attitude down to his level. This is done because he is so broken. He is so maniacal. He is strategic in how he does it. Anything you think you can say to reach him for compassion, help, or love has already been figured into his twisted equation. This is a game to him.

Drained – You will feel constantly stressed, exhausted, or influx and may not understand why. The narcissist draining you emotionally and is draining your energy and good vibes. The narcissist does not want you to have anything that is good because the narcissist does not have these things (so why should you or anyone else). The narcissist will drain you emotionally, energetically, spiritually, financially, sexually, and any other way the narcissist can personally hurt and destroy your inner being and inner peace.

Drama – Narcissists say they "don't like drama." This is another one of his lies. The narcissist loves drama. He thrives in creating drama. He feeds off drama. The narcissist does not care about other's drama. He is focused on the drama he creates and the drama in which he gets involved. He is interested in perpetuating emotional drama. Drama is not love. Your love will not be returned through any romantic dramatic fantasy. Go no contact to stop the drama monster.

Dysfunctional – From my experience, and from my research, it appears the narcissist is a severely damaged person with a warped, maladjusted background. Any type of relationship you have with a narcissist will be an unbalanced one. The narcissist is not your soulmate. The narcissist is not anyone's soulmate. Inherently, the narcissist knows this, so the narcissist destroys everyone emotionally in his path. The narcissist will attempt to make you feel as though you are not good enough for anyone. Truth be told, the narcissist is the one who is not good enough for anyone. People will see through the narcissist's dysfunction. It may take weeks, months, years, decades, but it will happen. The only thing you need to be concerned about is your well-being, your emotions, your reactions. Do not react to the crazymaking of the narcissist or his flying monkeys. The game for the narcissist is to rope you into responding to gaslight you, bait and bash you.

E

Education – The narcissist will try to sabotage your efforts in earning an education or self-improvement. He will interrogate you, belittle you, and need you during times you should be studying or working. Oh, you cannot study, or work in front of the narcissist because you are not paying attention to what the narcissist wants you to pay attention to or even to the narcissist himself. He will accuse you of being rude and ignoring him. He will accuse you of being self-absorbed. You will be accused of having an affair with the teacher or trying to impress the teacher/study group/other students. He will complain your studies are more important than him.

Eggshells – You are always going to be worried and with a slight scared feeling because of the fragile ego of the narcissist. If the fragile eggshell ego is at all annoyed by anything you do, it's as if you broke the eggshell and the narcissist rage once again begins.

Ego – From my experience and research, the narcissist has a fragile ego. He is not strong, not secure. He is very fragile. The narcissist builds or strengthens his ego by belittling you and destroying your healthy self-worth and a healthy ego. The narcissist concerns only about himself and his needs. The narcissist is self-ego driven.

Egocentricity – From my experience, the narcissist has no regard for other people or their feelings. A narcissist is fabulous at faking concern and regard especially if it suits the agenda of the narcissist. This toxic person only concerned about his own needs, feelings, and how others see/perceive him.

Elevates – The narcissist elevates nonissues to minor issues to full blown out arguments. A healthy relationship elevates you emotionally. A toxic relationship elevates a confused state.

Emotional vampire – The narcissist, a person with narcissistic traits or features, a person who is toxic, or the person who is simply a jerk is an emotional vampire. These types of people cannot feel empathy towards others; you are no exception. These types of people are dangerous to your emotional well-being. You will feel emotionally drained, exhausted after dealings with a narcissist, or someone who exhibits narcissistic behaviors. These toxic people are draining the positivity from you. You will feel your proverbial light starting to dim . . . because inside of you it is dimming. If you are, out of the ordinary, feeling low, depressed, anxious, ashamed, guilty, worthless, and you are not sure why, then realize that the person with whom you are in a relationship has either overtly or covertly planted these self-doubting, worry thoughts in you. It is worse when you know the narcissist is causing the emotional pain, but you have been conditioned to deny it. Your subconscious knows and is telling you. Honor this inner voice. You need to leave the relationship with the emotional vampire, a toxic human being immediately. Go not contact. Seek help for your depression.

Emotional withholding – This is a manipulation used by the narcissist to bring about pain to punish, and to control the target (that would be you). The narcissist will "shut down" or pout while giving you the silent treatment. Sometimes you know why you are being punished, other times it's a mystery the narcissist will not tell you and leave you wondering, worrying, internal questioning, and just dangling in the wind until the narcissist is ready to speak (cause a problem). This could be a withholding of affection, sex, attention. You name it. Whatever your weakness is, the narcissist will manipulate you with it. It's painful. It's emotional torture. When you realize this is not normal, you must leave the relationship. It will happen again and again and again. It will never get better. You will need to seek help to recover from narcissistic abuse.

Emotionally distant – The narcissist is detached. He is unable to form real connections. The narcissist is emotionally distant. The narcissist will never be authentically engaged with you. The narcissist may even tell you he never really loved you . . . even after 30 years of marriage. It was all a lie. That he married you "because you were there." If you are constantly asking, "Do you love me?" "Do you really love me?" "Do you even like me?" Or you constantly have that "alone" feeling in the relationship, even when you are sitting beside him, this is your intuition speaking, maybe screaming, to you. Listen to your intuition. Most likely, you're not being "needy." A narcissist will tell you that you're being needy. A person in love with you will make you feel loved and secure. A person in love with you has no problem telling you over and over and over again.

Emotionally drained – Walking on eggshells, being in a constant state of stress, living with anxiety and worry will cause you to be depleted emotionally. You will feel as though you have nothing more to give anyone . . . except for the narcissist. He will take, and take, and take until there is nothing left to give. You will end up crying a lot. You need to leave this creep and move on with your life by seeking help from a professional. You also need to connect with authentic, supportive, nurturing, compassionate people. They will be a breath of fresh air.

Emotionally immature – The narcissist is immature. The narcissist will appear to have normal emotional development, when in fact, it is an illusion. The narcissist is stunted and forever trapped, unable to progress from a lower level of emotional development. While others can move through the developmental phases, the narcissist never will be able to do so. The narcissist is not self-reflective. The narcissist does not believe anything is wrong with him. He does not see a need to be reflective or a need for growth and improvement. Normal emotionally developed people continue to improve and reflect to have a better life, a peaceful, joyful life.

Emotionally safe – The narcissist will make you feel emotionally safe in a short period of time. You will feel like this person really understands you and empathizes for you. This is an illusion. You are never going to be emotionally safe in a relationship with a narcissist.

Emotionally stunted – The narcissist is emotionally stuck, unable to progress through the normal and natural stages of development. He operates from a very immature level. You cannot fix him. You cannot help him. (Have you tried?) If you try to help him, he will turn it around on you, even if he has asked and "emotionally reached out to you for help," and blame you for it and chastise you for not helping him to the best of your abilities. He will use this to tear you apart as a failure as a person. You cannot fix him! Don't try! Go no contact for your own emotional well-being.

Empathy – Generally the narcissist was abused as a child. While this is sad, it does not mean you need to stick around with the adult who is now taking out narcissistic aggression out on you. Because of the abused endured as a young child, the narcissist lacks empathy. You will not receive empathy or compassion from this person. The narcissist is concerned only with himself, his needs, his wants, his desires, his standing, is life. To the narcissist, your life is not nearly as important as his life. Is that who you want to be by your side in an emergency? The narcissist is not concerned about you. He will help all others and leave you standing by yourself because he wants to look good. He's not helping in an emergency to be helpful. He's helping for his own ego. The narcissist is driven by his own ego.

Empowerment – The narcissist hates when his targets/victims heal and become empowered. Becoming empowered is your only (and most meaningful) revenge against your narcissistic abuser. Trying to show the world that he is a narcissist is pointless. He will bait and bash you. He will call you crazy and paint you out to be jealous or pathetic. Go no contact. Ignore the flying monkeys (do not engage with them). Get help in recovering from narcissistic abuse.

Empty – There is something "missing" with the narcissist and you can't quite figure it out. The narcissist may even tell you he's empty and devoid of feeling. That's your cue to turn and run.

Enables – Allows something to occur. A victim will enable the narcissist's behavior to avoid conflict either in private or in public. A victim will also allow the narcissist's behavior because she will explain it away in her head (or to others if they see it). The victim lives in denial.

Entitled – Believes he can do/have/take/participate in whatever he wants whenever he wants and will go to extreme measures to do so. The narcissist will use control of others to fulfill his wants and desires. The narcissist uses control of others to get what he believes he is entitled to have. The narcissist won't necessarily do the dirty work himself; he will have you or someone else do it for him. The narcissist is afraid of being told "no." Coward.

Envy – The narcissist envies most everyone else; yet, has contempt for them and despises them. The narcissist lives in a bizarre world of dissatisfaction and not being able to be fulfilled.

Envy issues – The narcissist is a jealous human being and very insecure. The narcissist is envious of everything about you. This does not endear him to you. His envy of you makes him want to tear you down and put you in your place. The narcissist finds satisfaction in putting people in their places.

Escalates – The narcissist escalates seemingly unimportant topics into all-out war. If you find yourself involved in this type of dialog, realize that you have been targeted by a narcissist. It will not get better. You will never be able to voice your concern over any topic that might trigger an escalation. You don't really want to live like that. Leave the toxic person and do not return to him regardless of the tricks and promises made. A narcissist will pull out all the stops to gain your trust and heart early in the relationship. It will create havoc on your emotions should you progress in the relationship.

Evidence – The narcissist likes to gather evidence against you to use against you in arguments, and publicly. (Seriously, he is a jerk.) He will get the evidence from you, from others by talking behind your back and creating scenarios to set you up. The narcissist is a master of strategy, baiting and bashing, provoking and blaming as well as overall crazymaking to belittle you and make you seem inferior to him.

Evolved – The narcissist is not evolved. The narcissist does not want you to grow or become evolved either. The narcissist will belittle and degrade you for wanting to improve yourself. If this occurs with anyone in your life, cut them loose. They are not supportive.

Exaggerates – Oh the narcissist magnifies everything from sickness, wellness, finances, jobs, cars, accomplishments, to problems, or failures. The lies he tells you and about you, and so on. Side note: This is unlike when you first meet someone and you (or they) exaggerate here and there to impress someone. That is normal. The abnormal narcissist exaggerates everything to an extreme.

Excuses – The narcissist lies. He makes up excuses that he expects, almost demands, you believe. If you do not believe his lies, he will question your character. He will demand-ask in a mean and hateful way, "So you think I am a liar?" (The answer is, "yes!")

Expectations – The narcissist will say your expectations of the relationship are too high (following the rapid love bombing and wooing used on you). The narcissist will purposefully make you feel confused.

■ The narcissist will have unreasonable expectations for you to achieve in pleasing him. This will be in helping him, doing things properly to his pleasing, expectations to constantly validating the narcissist, and acknowledging everything the narcissist does. Once you begin trying to please a narcissist, you will never be able to give enough of anything. You will be trapped in a cycle of unfulfilled expectations by the narcissist and the narcissist being mean to you because you were unable to meet these unreasonable expectations. The narcissist is an emotionally-unevolved bully. Go no contact immediately. You will never ever please a narcissist.

Explain – You will be constantly explaining what it is you meant because he will have taken whatever you did or said the "wrong" way. Your intentions, words, deeds may be innocent, good, or positive. That doesn't matter; the abuser will take twist them.

Explanations – You will be covering for him making up reasons and stories for him and to his benefit. This will only add to your denial and will ink you further into his web.

Explosive – You never know when the narcissist is going to go from a normal, calm state to one that is scary like a raging volcano. This explosion could be directed toward you, toward a server, a cashier, coworker, or . . . you name it.

Exploitive – The narcissist will find a weakness and use it unfairly against you. The narcissist will turn a situation into something unfavorable to expose your weakness or threaten to expose your weakness, to benefit in some way and to gain control over you. Being exploitive is all about gaining the upper hand and the never-ending need for the narcissist to feel superior over his target.

Exposing the narcissist – Once you realize who it is you are dealing with, you will want to tell everyone, convince everyone this person is a narcissist. Don't bother. The narcissist beat you to it using his innate strategy long, long ago. The narcissist knows how to behave in front of certain people. The narcissist knows how to gaslight you to make you feel and appear crazy. The narcissist knows how to paint you in a negative light and relishes the opportunity to do so. The narcissist will call upon his flying monkeys to help with his mission of destroying you. My advice to you is when you realize you are with a narcissist, you shouldn't bother explaining yourself or trying to prove anything to anyone—you will only get hurt. You simply need to leave the relationship and seek help for narcissistic abuse, and for improving your self-worth. Note: Like I said, there will be people who will not believe you and will even blame you for the demise of the relationship. You need to realize he has his own internal issues. Do not explain yourself to those people. Let them fade to black.

Extending the cycle – The narcissist finds ways to continue the cycle of abuse while you are in the relationship, and even when you have left the relationship. The narcissist will find reasons and ways to contact you: emergencies, illnesses, deaths, events, memories, and so on. Sometimes the narcissist is aggressive with you, the target. Sometimes it is more covert and underhanded in a stealth, "never saw it coming" manner. This means you must be vigilant in your own mental health and physical safety well-being by not engaging with the narcissist and by holding firm to going no contact. The narcissist is not emotionally available to help you in any way. The narcissist only wants to dominate you. Remain in no contact.

F

Faithful – Nope. Pass. The narcissist has a stable of "others" he taps into play whenever he feels like it. You might even be one of the "others" to some other person and you do not even know it. Fidelity is to a narcissist as an anchor is to a drowning person.

False mask – The narcissist wears a mask of charming lies. He is a wolf in sheep's clothing. When the mask comes off, you will see the abusive monster and wonder what the heck happened. Get out of this toxic relationship and go no contact.

Family – The narcissist may not even like his own family, or relatives; but, he will expect you to do all sorts of things for his family/relatives. He will expect you to purchase all the cards, and gifts. He will expect you to handle the arrangements with them. He will expect you to sit with them. He, on the other hand, is too busy playing his video games, on his smartphone with his girlfriend, too busy exercising, or doing whatever it is he wants to do. The narcissist wants the illusion that he almost, sort of cares about them. He doesn't. It is an act. The same goes for your family. He will use them for trips, vacations, presents . . . whatever he can get, even "large bags filled with cash." (No, he was not joking. That is what he wanted and expected from my family. He even was so bold to say it to their faces. Like me, they gave him what he wanted to keep him happy. That was our big mistake.) Narcissists are bold. They will tell you WHO they really are. You just have to listen.

Fantasy – The narcissist is delusional. The narcissist's make-believe world is a fantasy. The narcissist will think he deserves whatever it is the narcissist imagines. If the narcissist doesn't have these things, you will be blamed (as will the children, pets, co-workers, family, and friends).

Fantasy world – The narcissist often uses drugs, alcohol, porn, affairs, sexual conquests, money, food, and other addictions to hide the narcissist's extremely low self-esteem. He cannot outrun who he truly is no matter how hard he tried. When faced with the truth about himself, he will blame someone else and make it someone else's fault. He is always ready with an excuse.

Fast – The narcissist attaches quickly and love bombs. This is a trick. The narcissist wants you to commit quickly. The narcissist speeds the pace of the relationship, skipping over the dating and the wooing. The narcissist doesn't necessarily want to treat you well and romance you for the long haul. Instead, the narcissist front loads affection, sweet nothings, cards, presents, texts, phone calls, messages, attention. Should you want to slow the relationship down or take a breath, the narcissist will use guilt on you. After he has you, you are "suffocating him." He will breadcrumb you. He will give you just enough attention to make you hang on. You are a valueless object to the narcissist.

Fault – You are always at fault for everything. The narcissist will blame you for all his shortcomings, including his career, his finances, bank account, his bills, his home, his friends, your friends, his motivation or lack thereof, and so on. If someone blames you for something unjustly or blames you over a bizarre topic, turn and run and do not look back. Go no contract from the narcissist.

Favor – The narcissist will request, as well as demand, many favors from you. If you fail to yield to the requests, the narcissist will make you feel as though there is something wrong with you and that you are incompetent. (There is nothing wrong with you. It's the narcissist. The narcissist has the major personality disorder—not you.) If you disagree in wanting to do the favor requested—WATCH OUT!

Fear – If you are feeling nervous, worried, or afraid of interactions with your narcissist (or contemplating having to discuss something with the narcissist), it is time to seek help. Healthy, loving, supportive relationships do not trigger a sense of fear, fright, worry, panic. You need to go no contact immediately. The narcissist equates fear with power, control, and respect. Most partners would be glad their partner is not afraid of them. The narcissist wants fear from you. Forcing you into submission does not equal respect.

■ You may be even too afraid to call the police for a variety of reasons. If fear is involved in a relationship, along with physical abuse, call the police. Get a PFA—protection from abuse—if you are in fear of your safety. Do this before the narcissist does to bait, blame, and bash you with his manufacture red evidence . . . or simply lies about you to obtain protection from you. The narcissist does not care who he hurts: spouses, children, pets . . . anyone under his narcissistic control.

Fearful – The narcissist is afraid of his real identity being displayed for all to see. The narcissist is afraid of being exposed. Image management is what the narcissist practices the most. I'd say image management the narcissist's true religion.

Feelings – First, your feelings don't matter. Second, if your feelings and opinions differ from his, he will make you feel like a bad, awful human being for being alive. (I was scream-asked, "What's wrong with your DNA?" by someone intent on hurting my feelings. This was screamed at me as I stood silently and did not engage because I did something the narcissist did not like. This was used as an opportunity to degrade, berate, and shame me when I proudly obtained a new job. I could not do anything right.)

Financial abuse – The narcissist wants to take as much as the narcissist can from those around him. The narcissist will take from you. The narcissist will control your money. This happens because you were manipulated by a narcissist. You will try to please the narcissist and prove your worth to the narcissist. You will want to prove your loyalty to the narcissist (this may even be demanded by the narcissist). What proves your loyalty more than money? That's the line of bull the narcissist will trick you into believing. Or perhaps he will manipulate you into believing you are incapable of handling finances so he will do it for you "to take care of you." That is another line of bull! The toxic manipulator is a liar who steals, empties bank accounts to 19 cents, exercises stock options, and has secret bank accounts of his own. (Ask me how I know. My former spouse did that.) Of course, the narcissist could claim to be broke and you are the only one he would trust to ask for money. Um, no! There is no one else who would give the arrogant manipulator money. If you've given passwords, you need to change them immediately. Cancel your credit cards and order new ones. Talk to the bank officers. Request new checking routing account. If you need to, involve the police.

Fix – You cannot repair a narcissist into an emotionally healthy human being. The narcissist may ask you for your special help because no one else understands him like you. The narcissist may attempt to convince you that you're the only one he's ever actually trusted so it must be you who helps repair him. He will admit he's "broken" or "damaged" in order to manipulate your people-pleasing nature. Don't fall for it. You absolutely, without a shadow of a doubt, cannot help a narcissist. Do not respond to his fake pleas for help. They are lies and manipulations to get another narcissistic fix from you. (A narcissistic fix is different than your desire to "fix" this lost soul. He's not lost. He's a sneaky snake manipulator.)

Flaws – While the narcissist doesn't think he has any flaws (and certainly won't acknowledge flaws—he will blame them on someone else), he is happy to learn what your flaws are and exploit them for his own need to feel superior over you.

Flips out on a dime – You never know what will trigger the narcissist into a rage, meltdown, or volcanic eruption.

Flirting – The narcissist presents himself as gregarious, charming, and delightful. Should you behave in a polite manner to someone (a co-worker, friend, and random wait staff), you will be accused of flirting and accused of wanting to be with that person you are being accused of flirting with. A whole issue will be made of it. It's ridiculous and pathetic of the narcissist, but it shows the narcissist's insecurity and insensitivity and that the narcissist really does not have any respect for you whatsoever.

Flying monkeys – These are psychologically dependent people who, for some reason, need the approval the narcissist. They do the dirty work for the narcissist because they are puppets to the narcissist and because they, too, enjoy drama and creating a mess. Flying monkeys are spineless. They only have the courage or a spine when they are in a group of like-minded puppets. The flying monkeys may be narcissists as well. They expect your narcissist to defend their exploits as well. Generally, narcissists will defend each other because they see value in doing that for the narcissist because they too have something to hide: who they really are.

Forgive yourself – You need to pick yourself up (with the help of a specialist and a supportive network), dust yourself off, and forgive yourself for mistakes you made with friends and family while under the narcissist's control.

Forgiveness – You will find yourself forgiving the narcissist repeatedly—in your mind because he does not think he did anything wrong. The narcissist will never apologize or ask for forgiveness because the narcissist doesn't think he did anything wrong. The narcissist can righteously justify his actions as well as easily place blame on you and/or anyone else he feels inferior. The narcissist will dig his heels in and create an entirely fake story in which he adopts. This story will be used against you as proof of his righteousness. It's a frustrating manipulation and lie game the narcissist plays.

Forthcoming – A narcissist, and a jerk in general will use avoidance and lies to hide from being available and accessible. The narcissist will use many tactics to steer clear of giving you a firm decision on most anything including commitments with you. He needs to have his time open in case something better comes along. He also wants to play with your emotions. Leaving you wondering is fun for him and produces anxiety, worry, and tears for you.

Fragile – The narcissist wants you raw, vulnerable, and filled with worry, anxiety, and self-doubt. You need to break free from this abuser and seek help from a specialist. Go no contact. Do not take him back, or engage with his (or his flying monkeys) crazymaking after the breakup.

■ The narcissist is a fragile being. He's had a lifetime of learning to cover it up and hide it. It surfaces though, and it surfaces often. When it surfaces, it's scary. He's trying to hurt you the same way he feels inside: broken and desperate. Boo hoo. That's his issue with his therapist, not your issue. No one should take their insecurities and issues out on you. You cannot repair or nurture this emotional vampire.

Fragment – The narcissist damages you emotionally to separate you from others, and even including removing you from yourself so you are easier to control and dominate. (Meaning, you will become self-doubting and always looking for direction . . . from the controlling narcissist.) It makes one feel empty, lost, confused, and sad.

Fraud – The narcissist wears a mask. The persona the narcissist first shows you is a fake, a phony, a liar, unethical, a fraud. Once you see behind the mask, the nice mask is gone and you are now looking at the real person.

Friends – The narcissist will make fun of you and your friends (but not necessarily to their faces). He may be charming to them directly, but behind the scenes, he belittles you because of your friends and family. The narcissist will encourage you, threaten you, force you, and manipulate you to lose them. This is different from a concerned mate wanting you to put some distance between yourself and someone who is legitimately self-destructing, and it would be better for your safety to not cut ties. The narcissist wants to isolate you from your friends and family.

Friends with benefits (it's a trick) – The narcissist may trick you into believing that you are dating exclusively or are in a mutually exclusive relationship. YOU ARE NOT EVER EXCLUSIVE with a narcissist.

Frighten – The narcissist uses fear to make you worry, self-doubt, become anxious, and to make you bend to his will.

Frustration – The tactics and manipulations used by the narcissist are often frustrating on the target/victim/partner. If you are often feeling frustrated by this person, you need to take a step back and ask yourself why you are allowing someone to frustrate you so much.

Fulfilled – Because the narcissist is emotionally empty, the narcissist is rarely ever satisfied. He wants more, must have more, attain more, achieve more, go higher in the company, more muscles, more distance in running/biking (whatever sport), go faster, more women, more conquests, more in his stable, more challenges, more ideas he does not follow through on, and have more money. Watch your bank account ladies. He will take your savings so he can have "more."

Fun – Forget fun after the love bombing and the narcissist has you in his clutches. The narcissist will be the only one having fun in the relationship. The narcissist's fun is manipulating you and hurting you. Then, blaming you for causing drama. You are not allowed to have fun with anyone else. Should you have a night, or even an afternoon, or an innocent breakfast with a friend or friends, the narcissist will be jealous. The narcissist will make you feel awful for going and having a pleasant time with friends. The narcissist will punish you for having fun by going out trolling for his next fix. He will go to the extreme and use the excuse that you went out so he will too. His gong out is meant to be a punitive experience and is intended to teach you a lesson.

Futile – The narcissist will frustrate you to no end. You will go around and around and around on ridiculous topics which are arguments created by the toxic narcissist. He will not let you win. He is intent on hurting and destroying you. There is no middle ground with the narcissist.

G

Gaslighting – The narcissist will invalidate your emotions, feelings, and actual events that occurred by telling you you're crazy, you take things too seriously, you're trying to cause drama, you are too sensitive, that you are making things up that didn't happen (narcissists do that all the time to justify confusing and unkind actions), and will tell you your perception is off. He will eventually tell you that you are a narcissist (gaslighting, blame shifting).

■ 1. Don't confuse your own strength and empowerment with being a narcissist

■ 2. Used to confuse and distort the truth

Generalizations – The narcissist makes broad and unclear statements to throw you off balance. He will generalize the things you say or the events that have occurred to his benefit. The generalizations will be so twisted you feel as though you must "be better" and "do better" so there are no perceived mistakes in the future. There will always be generalizations with just about everything you do twisted in a manner to make you feel bad so the narcissist and his fragile, low self-esteem ego feels superior.

Getting away with it – The narcissist's primary goal is to get away with whatever is on the narcissist's agenda. When you realize this, go no contact immediately. The narcissist is a manipulator and a liar. There is no reason to contact the narcissist. (You will be told you are crazy, wrong, and end up being blamed if you contact the narcissist, or want to talk about it to highlight an issue in the relationship. Forget it. The narcissist does not care about the issue and does not care about you.

Ghosting – Do it! It's a form of your no contact rule that you need to implement. You probably already know what this tactic is because the narcissist has already used it on you. Ghosting is the sudden, and without notice, reason, explanation, withdrawal of communication thereby ending a relationship. I suggest you implement this practice as a protective form of self-healing. (No, doing this does not make you a narcissist if you are ending communication with a toxic individual.) If you give the narcissist a "reason" in order to help him improve or hope he gets it, you are kidding yourself. The narcissist does not care why you are ending a relationship. He is more concerned that you are developing self-worth. He hates that. If you provide reasons, he will attempt to persuade and convince you not to end it with him. You might become weak and give him another chance (do not do it). Then he will turn around when you are feeling comfortable and ghost you. He is putting you in your place. (Uh-oh: how dare you try to regain your self-worth and become empowered.) Do not give the narcissist your power. Keep your power!

Gifts – The narcissist will give gifts to love bomb you and woo you. The narcissist might provide gifts to you after the narcissist has done something dastardly, mean, silent treatment and is in that phase of "rescuing" you. Let me give you this piece of advice: do not sell your soul for something shiny or for a present. You don't need it. What you need to do is heal and improve your self-esteem and self-worth. The gifts will be used against you. You will be called names like "greedy" or "unappreciative." The gifts come with strings and have an agenda.

Giver – Most likely you are a giver of yourself . . . too much so. A giver is an empath or empathetic person. A giver is a narcissist's twisted dream come true. The narcissist may even trick you, or guilt you, into buying him gifts. You may even go broke trying to please him. Go no contact and figure out why you are overly giving and why it is you want people to like you to the degree you are handing over your integrity, your grace over to some schmuck—even a sexy, charming schmuck. A narcissist is a schmuck. You can and will do better. Walk away and don't look back!

Go no contact – For your own mental and emotional healing, as well as your physical safety, you cannot engage, contact, reply, or respond to the narcissist for any reason what so ever. You must block the narcissist, his friends, and the flying monkeys from all social media. You must change all your passwords (all of them), change your email, block his texting and phone number, and change your credit card information. It might be proactive to inform the bank that you are going no contact from a toxic person who likely has your banking information. Do your protective due diligence. If you have children, there are protected court ordered websites that are created for parent communication focusing solely only on the children. Going no contact is very difficult. Consult a specialist for assistance. You need to also enlist a group of friends to help you through it. Be clear very with them. Tell them you are going no contact. (If they are truly good friends who saw through the mask of the narcissist, they will be so relieved for you.) Tell them you are going to have many moments of weakness and times you feel as though you are crawling out of your skin. Explain to your support group that those are the times you are going to need their help. The narcissist has chipped away at your self-worth. You need them while you rebuild it.

Goalposts – "Moving the goalposts" is a tactic used by the narcissist to be disgusted, displeased, unhappy with you and to create a situation—to get the narcissistic fix of putting you in your place by making you feel inferior, and to punish you. Moving the goalposts is what the narcissist does to create confusion. The narcissist will find reasons to be disgusted and frustrated by you and your efforts. Give up and get out of this relationship. You will never please this person, nor will this person ever be truly happy with you . . . or himself. The narcissist is emotionally void.

Gratified – If you think you have seen a glimmer of happiness, gratification, or joy in seeing you lose social standing, losing it while being engaged by a narcissist, or seeing you lose your sense of self, you are correct. The narcissist enjoys the feeling of seeing this happen and hearing about this happen. When you catch the gratification of the narcissist, do not explain it away. See it for what it is and leave this toxic human being. You need to be with someone who elevates and nurtures you.

Greedy – The narcissist is selfish, possessive, and self-indulgent. The narcissist is a taker. The narcissist wants as much as he can possibly get, or take, from everyone around him. The narcissist comes from a place of emptiness and lack, therefore, the narcissist tries to compensate by taking (and taking and taking, and taking) from others. The narcissist will deplete you emotionally, financially, and in all ways.

Grieving – Regardless of how long you were in a relationship with the narcissist, you will experience a grief and loss. You know going "no contact" is the absolute right thing to do, but you will go through the stages of grief. Remain in "no contact" mode. White-knuckle through it if you have to, but do not contact the narcissist.

Grunts – The narcissist can't be bothered to use words to speak like an adult; or, may think it is perfectly appropriate to communicate with grunts and odd sounds. You are expected to decipher the meaning of the grunting sounds. Some grunts and sounds are passive aggressive. Some grunts and sounds are aggressive. In my opinion from my experience and from the research, grunting is a clear sign of the narcissist's immaturity and developmental level.

Guilt – The narcissist uses tone as well as words to instill guilt into your psyche. It's immature and childish. The narcissist is unable to behave like a rational human being for long periods of time. Be wary! Guilt is a transition tactic into a full-blown tantrum or rage.

H

Happiness – If you are with a narcissist, forget about true happiness. The emotion you will feel is fear and worry most of the time. The narcissist is not concerned about your happiness at all. The narcissist only wants to dominate and control you. Your happiness is not of concern to the narcissist. You need to leave an unhappy relationship that is toxic to your psyche. To have a fulfilling life, you need to begin with happiness and self-love which will increase your self-worth. Seek help from a specialist.

Happy – The narcissist is discontented if he sees someone else happy; especially for reasons unknown to him. The narcissist feels he is the only one who can bring happiness to others . . . including you. One of the primary reasons he is discontented is because he is jealous. He is emotionally void so he does not know or even understand true happiness. He is jealous of others who experience delight and joy. Should the narcissist see you in a happy state, he will surely make a snide, cutting remark to discredit you and your good mood.

Harasses – The narcissist will bother you, belittle you, and pester you into bending to his will. This can be both an overt, in your face type of harassment, or the covert harassment in which various forms of manipulation are used to harass you. Should you finally muster up your self-worth and courage and leave the narcissist, you will be harassed by either the narcissist himself or by his flying monkeys. Harassment is illegal. Document the harassment by calling the police, reporting it to your attorney, reporting the harassment to a counselor, professional, and telling the courts. Share your story. Expose the harassment and bring it to the light of day.

Harboring – The narcissist holds onto grudges to remind you that you are inferior. Often times the narcissist will bring up events from long ago that displeased him, or events that you thought were in the past and solved. He uses these negative harbored, pent-up anger, feelings and throws them at you to blindside you, throw you off balance and put you on the defense.

Harem – The narcissist has many women. The narcissist juggles the women. The narcissist uses women. You are just one of many. This is also called the narcissist's "stable." The narcissist will eventually compare you to them in a twisted, manipulative tactic called triangulation. You deserve better. Go no contact immediately.

Harsh – The narcissist's treatment of you is harsh. It will leave you feeling insecure and inferior.

Haughty – The narcissist thinks he is better than everyone else and will behave in such a manner. It's impolite and rude. The narcissist doesn't care though. It's a game to the narcissist.

Haunting – You broke up with the narcissist. You are going no contact. The monkey mind is chattering away with negativity haunting your mind, telling you to cave, reinforcing the unkind and unpleasant things he said to you and tricked you into believing. Seek help in reducing and eliminating the negative chatter in your mind. It makes the healing slightly easier.

Head spinning – Your head will be in an almost constant state of confusion, worry, and fog when trying to figure out why the narcissist is mad at you "this time." You will be in an almost constant state of worry over trying to do the right thing to not upset the precious prince.

Healing – Go "no contact" to heal. This is a priority for your mental and emotional well-being. You need to heal. The narcissist will behave as though he is the wounded victim and is healing too. Here's the truth to that: No they are not. He may be wounded but you will never really know the truth and he is not in any process of healing. A narcissist does not look inward; therefore, there is nothing to heal or even improve within the narcissist. The narcissist does know what to say, though, to trick you into thinking the narcissist has a heart. Forget that thought. Go no contact and don't look back. Seek help for healing after narcissistic abuse.

Heartless – The narcissist does not love you. The narcissist does not love you. The narcissist does not love you. The narcissist does not love you. You are not soulmates. He is not "your love." You are something to be controlled.

Help – Narcissistic abuse is a real thing and a real problem. This is unlike a past relationship. You will need help navigating your emotions, taming the monkey mind, learning coping skills, understanding triggers, and perhaps even working through PTSD. Surviving narcissistic abuse takes a village . . . and going no contact from your narcissist. A narcissist is an abusive person.

Hero – The narcissist loves being the hero. (Even when he isn't.) Even the smallest tasks, he will use as victoriously saving of the day.

Heroine – You cannot rescue him. You need to be your own hero (because he is not going to be there for you). Have fun with your life. You only get one.

Hierarchy – There's a hierarchy of importance to the narcissist. You are at the bottom.

HIPAA – Health Insurance Portability and Accountability Act. HIPPA protects your medical information privacy. You must make sure to change your "in case of emergency," remove his name: gyms, dentist, eye doctor, medical, psychological, pharmacy, chiropractor, spas . . . anywhere you write an "in case of emergency" name. If you don't, he will have access to all your appointments, and medical information.

His story – The toxic person changes his history. He will tell you that his former wife (wives), girlfriends were crazy, or controlling. (He will use the word, "controlling" a lot in his conversations. This is a clue! He is telling you who he is.) He is a victim of theirs. His tale of woe is long and he always has the short end of the stick. It is like junior high. The same things he has said about them, he will say about you to the others in his stable.

Holidays and special events – Without a shadow of a doubt, the narcissist will cause a problem, some sort of drama (like cheating, leaving you, hurting you, ghost you, and so on), blaming you for whatever, or even a rage. The narcissist cannot stand to see others happy and have fun. The narcissist will make your life miserable if you do not do exactly as he wants (sometimes even if you do—he will find a reason to become/maintain his miserable attitude). The narcissist will even say with a degrading tone that he will do whatever he wants to do anyways and you will not tell him what to do. The narcissist will break up with you right before each holiday and birthday. The narcissist will even have the nerve to blame you for the breakup. It is not your fault. The narcissist is the only one to blame because the narcissist caused the drama because of lack of attention and because of the need to get the narcissistic fix on victims. The narcissist is so immature. The narcissist will find coal in his Christmas stocking. My best advice to you: have back up plans for holidays and special events ready. Then GO NO CONTACT. This is an absolute must! If he will ruin your holidays or special event once, he WILL DO IT AGAIN . . . and AGAIN! Block him from all social media and change your passwords. You may want to cancel your credit cards and order new ones.

■ Easter morning, as I was in my closet picking out my outfit, my former spouse told me he was leaving me . . . again . . . for his married co-worker mistress. He spent the week professing his love for me and "apologizing to me" for beating me a week and a half earlier. I decided to end the pain by ending my life. I began to wake up in the hospital three days later to his love bombing and breadcrumbing. Then the flip of his personality occurred along with his provoking and gaslighting to bait and bash me. Know this: cruelty and crazymaking will happen during special occasions.

Hoops – You must jump through hoops to be pleasing to the narcissist, and to prove your worth and your value. Stop it. You're perfect. The narcissist doesn't care about you anyway and is only going to belittle you no matter what you do.

Hostage – Even when you are ready to break free, and want to break free, you may feel like you are held hostage by him emotionally. You may feel paralyzed. He has implanted this in you. You will be FINE without him! In my situation, I couldn't see a way out. I couldn't see tomorrow. Everything was black . . . because I was at the black hole of depression. There is always help. Step one: Get out! Don't wait any longer. Seek help from trusted friends and family. Call a specialist to help you recover from abuse. Follow through with going no contact.

Hostile – From what I have experienced, the narcissist's true personality is one of hostility, anger, and aggression. He can hide it, contain it only for so long. The hostility will surface eventually, maybe to get that all-important fix, and then might be controlled for a while. If you are with a narcissist long enough, you might be able to track when it is going to happen to try to make things as pleasing and pleasant as possible. When the narcissist wants a fix, he will find any reason, even a small one, in which to flip out to get his fix.

Humiliation – To make you feel inferior (and to make the narcissist feel superior), the narcissist will embarrass you in both public and private. When you say something about it, you will be called oversensitive, too sensitive, and be told you can't take a joke. The narcissist may also use your emotional hurt to project issues onto you and may even start an argument. If you are involved with anyone like this, you need to leave the relationship immediately. Go no contact. Seek help in narcissistic abuse recovery.

Humility – The narcissist is outstanding at faking humbleness, modesty if it suits his agenda. For example, ministers, pastors, highly religious individuals may be narcissists publicly hiding behind a fake persona. The empath in the narcissist's life knows exactly who he is, but dares not to expose him. The narcissist has the empath under control. The narcissist's flying monkeys are there to back up the narcissist should someone pull the mask off his being.

Hunt – The narcissist is always on the hunt for his next conquest. Do you think you're his one and only? Maybe for short periods of time. In reality, you're not special to him. You're one of many.

Hurt and rescue – The narcissist will hurt you. He will withhold affection, or use the silent treatment. You become sad, distraught, depressed. Then the narcissist will "rescue" you from his punishment. Will you be relieved? Will you be happy you're reunited? Will you be happy he has shifted the blame on you so you feel bad about yourself and ultimately apologize so the narcissist will "forgive" you for your shifted wrongdoing? Is that how you want to live?

Hypersensitive – The toxic person believes everything he wants he should have immediately. He will become incensed and blame you for lack of goal attainment. This could be a job, travel destination, housing, and autos—superficial things. Image management is what the narcissist focuses on.

■ The narcissist will plant seeds of doubt in you creating worry and anxiety in you which will make you feel hypersensitive to him. Not only will he plant seeds of doubt in you and your accomplishments, he will plant seeds of doubt about your friends, family, co-workers, medical professionals, anyone you trust and come in contact with. (He will manipulate you into believing that all of them have an agenda and ulterior motives. He is the one with ulterior motives.)

Hypersensitive narcissist (also known as an introverted narcissist, covert narcissist, vulnerable narcissist, closet narcissist)

Hypocrite – The narcissist is self-serving and believes he is faultless. The narcissist believes he has no culpability his own actions. (Those actions are "caused" by someone else. The narcissist will blame YOU for things the narcissist chooses to do either by choice or through lack of control.) The narcissist will groom and condition you to become worried over making mistakes. The narcissist's bizarre logic will almost make sense that you are to blame for whatever the issue, when in reality, the issue, or the worst of it, should fall squarely on the shoulders of the narcissist. The narcissist will provoke you and then call you names to make you feel inferior. To the narcissist, someone else "made" the narcissist does what he did. The narcissist will point out all your mistakes, shortcomings, flaws, and faults. The narcissist neglects to acknowledge or realize, he has any issues whatsoever. Well, the narcissist will point the finger at you as being the narcissist's biggest flaw, mistake, and fault. You are always to blame (even when you're not.) The narcissist is like a chameleon. He says one thing, does another and has an outlandish set of rules you need to follow or you will be punished. Of course, the narcissist will call YOU a hypocrite repeatedly throughout the relationship. The narcissist is telling you what HE is when he does this. He is showing you who HE is.

I

Idealization/Devaluation – The narcissist love bombs you and builds you up with (false) kindnesses to pull you into his world. When you fall for it, the narcissist will then become bored with you and begin to devalue you. The idealization portion is a short, but incredibly intoxicating, period. The devaluation lasts as long as you remain in a relationship or have contact with the narcissist. He will never idealize you again. Your relationship is an illusion because the narcissist's idealization was an illusion. The narcissist is a composite of other people he is copying. He, himself, is an illusion. He has no personality of his own, except anger and deceit.

Ideas – Every idea the narcissist has is a "terrific" idea that he wants to follow through with and expects you to handle it . . . right now, right away. You have been trained by the narcissist to be helpful and have been conditioned to constantly prove your worth to the narcissist, so of course, you jump on the projects and ideas he has. You will spend hours, days, weeks, months on projects and research. He's not doing any of the work. He wants all the credit though. He is not doing any of the follow through for the project. He will throw problems into the mix constantly even though he has no idea of the work involved or the actual logistics or legality of what the narcissist wants to be accomplished. Then he is not going to do anything with the work you've done anyway. It is a game. It is a test. You are a resourceful person. Build your own empire and leave the narcissist in the past.

Identification – You may think you are involved with a narcissist. You may think if you talk about this with the person, that person gets help in not being a narcissist anymore. You might think you can help that person through to wellness. FORGET IT! First, if you think you are dating, or married to a narcissist, you very well could be. That person is clearly toxic nonetheless. You will do nothing to help by saying, "I think you are a narcissist. Let's get help in exploring this." This will be turned around on you to make you out be a narcissist. Yes, you "love" this person. The important piece you must know: this person does NOT love you. If you suspect the person you are involved with is a narcissist, then there is NO LOVE for you. There is no respect. There is no concern. There is only this twisted need to control the events, activities, thoughts, feelings you have. (That is not love.) You need to go no contact from this toxic person and seek help in healing.

Identifying – Time will show you who the narcissist is. Some things may seem normal, but then little things build up and increase. You will see who he is. There will be clues. He is stuck in his younger, less evolved developmental time.

Ignorant – The narcissist may be highly educated (or not); however, the things he will say and do will seem as if he has no manners or courtesy. The narcissist is ignorant because the narcissist is unable to control his behaviors and will go out of control because he's easily triggered. No amount of degrees hanging on his wall, or lack of, will justify being unkind, mean . . . or ignorant.

Ignore – The narcissist does not care about you. The narcissist does not care about your desires, hopes, dreams, and needs. After he has learned what your wishes, fantasies, and goals are, he uses them to exploit you and wound you. He will ignore you. He will ignore all your hopes and dreams as well. The narcissist simply wants to make you, another person, feel inferior. He does not love you. You are a challenge and a game.

Illusion – The narcissist's personality is an illusion. It's a composite of qualities he's seen in others. He uses these qualities to appear as attentive, caring, loving, fun, energetic, all the positive qualities he likely mirrored off of you while he is tricking you into his sick, sadistic relationship. His personality is an illusion. If you are under his control long enough, there will come a point that he will even tell you that it is an illusion. He thinks he has that much power over you. You will try to prove your worth and how your feelings are not an illusion so his feelings couldn't be either. Forget about trying to reason with that logic. The narcissist does not operate with logic, love, or emotion. The narcissist operates from some warped sense of self-created rules. The relationship was, indeed, an illusion; because the narcissist is a master illusionist. The narcissist's love for you was an illusion.

Image management – Of course everyone wants to put their best foot forward. For the narcissist, his image is the reason for his being. Image management is the narcissist's true religion.

Immature – The narcissist's developmental level is stunted; therefore, he is immature. The narcissist is immature and has low self-worth and high self-hatred. He wants to feel better by making others feel contempt as well.

Impatient – You will find the narcissist always waiting on you, even if you are usually on time. The narcissist is impatient. The narcissist will run late or not even show up if the activity is for you. Your events are unimportant to the narcissist. His activities, events, needs, desires always take precedence.

Imperious – Arrogant. The narcissist is arrogant. It is this arrogance where you will see the domineering, rude, overbearing, bossy behaviors.

Imply – The narcissist is famous for implying things to stay away from culpability on so many levels—from making plans with you to making you scared of his actions. The narcissist will imply threats, blackmail to throw you off, create worry, stress, and anxiety. The narcissist will use blame though when you remind him he said . . . Ah, ah, ah . . . Nope, he said nothing. Instead, he implied. You have been manipulated! You have been gaslighted. Fool me once . . . now get out of this twisted, toxic relationship.

Important – The narcissist is the most important person in the relationship. You are not important to the narcissist. You are an object for his narcissist fix. You are nothing more to make the narcissist feel better about himself. That's it. The narcissist must devalue you and make you feel unimportant for the narcissist to have feelings of superiority.

Imposing – The narcissist has no problem insisting you do things for him even if you are unable to due to scheduling, ethics, finances, family, and so on. The narcissist wants you to do what he wants when he wants even if you don't want to do it or cannot do it. It doesn't matter to him. He will shame you should you give your reasons for declining. (By the way, you should never feel obligated to give reasons to anyone.) The narcissist won't stand for a decline. He will attempt to force you into doing what he wants. Otherwise, you will be in for some punishments. (Then again, you might receive punishments anyway.)

Imposition – Anything and everything you ask of the narcissist is going to be "such" an imposition to him. He may do it, but boy oh boy will you know it. He will groan and moan, and make either underhanded or right out there in-your-face comments. Personally, I suffer from a food allergy. I would have a painful internal bloating attack, in which I feel like I wanted to be curled up in a ball and not move. I would ask the toxic person for an antacid tablet, or a bottle of water. Oh dear God. His agony of giving me assistance made me often think twice before asking for help (which is exactly what HE wants you to do). If I made the mistake of asking for both water, and a tablet, I was laughed at, made fun of, chastised, and questioned. Anything the narcissist does for someone is an imposition. The gloater will either endlessly tell others how he "had" to do the certain task, or will have you do it for him. (It's the least you could do after he handed you a bottle of water and an antacid when you thought your insides were going to burst.) The narcissist wants you to feel inferior and ashamed.

Impulsive – The narcissist is impulsive when it suits him . . . only him and in a way to elevate his status and/or to make himself feel superior over others including feeling superior over you.

Incompetent – Try as you might, you are not going to get it right. You will make honest mistakes. The narcissist will blow the mistakes out of proportion. He will belittle you and will chip away at your self-worth. The narcissist will look for mistakes. The narcissist will create them and make them up to make you feel inferior. You might even make a mistake because you are so worried. Stop worrying by getting rid of this nitpicker.

Inconsistent – The narcissist is inconsistent with his lies, stories, emotions, feelings for you, and so on. The narcissist is fake therefore he is not able to live a consistent life. The narcissist is picking and choosing qualities from other people. These qualities are not his own therefore the narcissist cannot form consistent behaviors. The narcissist is consistent at being inconsistent and inauthentic.

Inconvenient – Should you need medicine, help with a ladder, or a task you want to be completed, the narcissist will avoid helping you because it is such an inconvenience to him. He may do it, but at a cost to your psyche. He will laugh at you, make fun of you, belittle you, and shame you. He won't let you forget it either. If he manages to avoid helping you, he will blame you saying you didn't remind him, or you didn't bring it up. (How many times do you have to ask, for heaven's sake?) Do you need medicine from another room while you are feeling unwell? It's a struggle for the selfish narcissist to get off the couch to help you feel better. Should that happen to you, break up with this jerk? It will not get better.

Individualized – The narcissist's abuse toward you is unique to you. Each victim's abuse and manipulation is either slightly or vastly different from the last victim. It depends on your weaknesses and wounds and how the narcissist can manipulate you. No two victims are the same. The narcissist will tell you tales of how awful the last person in his life was (and you will take relief that you are nothing like that person). Here's the thing, the last victim most likely wasn't the culprit. The culprit is likely the person you're talking to. It is absolutely certain that the nasty things the narcissist is saying about his last victim, he will say about you too. You will have to get past that and not care what he and his flying monkeys say about you. Instead, get help in focusing on how to become empowered.

Inferior – The narcissist looks at you as less than, or as an underling. The narcissist will make you feel inferior, not worthy, and not good enough as if you are lacking something important in your personality and character and are not worthy of his affection.

■ The narcissist will make you feel inferior, will try to make you prove your worth to him. Don't fall for it.

Inferiority complex – The narcissist has very deeply rooted inferiority issues. All the mean and cruel behaviors he exacts on others are to cover up and disguise his own self-hate and inferiority issues. You cannot fix this. You cannot fix him! Not now. Not ever. Not with compassion. Not with attention. His inferiority complex is so ingrained there is nothing you can do, except to protect yourself by no longer being in the cycle of this toxic relationship. You deserve better than what the narcissist is doing to you because of his own personality disorder. Go no contact and seek help.

Inflated importance – The narcissist thinks he is better than everyone else. The narcissist believes his own line of baloney. The narcissist believes his everything is more important than everyone's "whatever." You are insignificant to the narcissist. You are there for his reasons and none of them are authentically good, or positive for you. Nor are the reasons for pure love. Oh no. He is not with you for love. Regardless of how long you have been together, or all you have done for him, the narcissist does not love you. He is with you because he found a weakness in you to exploit for whatever reasons he wants to make himself feel better. If it's monetary, then you better change the password to your banking, cancel your cards and order new ones. Protect yourself, protect your emotions from the narcissist, and protect your financial future from him as well.

Inner conversations with yourself – These are things you want to say to the narcissist. These are things you wish you could say to the narcissist. These are things you know you will never say to the narcissist because you know, at some level, he will turn the tables on you. You know at some level, having a voice or an opinion, will make everything so much worse. These are a red flag. When you start having conversations with him about how frustrated you are and you can picture him flipping out or making you feel bad in your own fantasy or imagination, you need to go no contact right away. If you have lost all hope that you cannot even have a nice conversation in your mind with him, oh honey, that is a huge red flag. You need character strengthening. If you have inner conversations that are arguments after having an argument with him, that is another red flag. You are not being heard by him. You will never be heard by him.

Inner wounds – The narcissist has unhealed pain that has nothing to do with you, that could have happened decades ago, which is why he is so twisted, mean, and manipulative. The more important piece for "inner wounds" is that YOU have inner unhealed wounds too. Your inner wounds have manifested into a sad piece, or several pieces, of you that are hurting. The narcissist's inner wounds have manifested into toxic emotional pollution. The narcissist is an attentive listener, at first, to find out what your hopes, dreams, fears, and wounds are. The narcissist will use those to tear you down, to threaten you, to belittle you, and to abuse you.

Innuendo – The narcissist makes suggestions. The narcissist says things without saying them to avoid accountability and to gaslight you with a double meaning. Innuendo is used to make you question if he really said what he said, really meant what he said. Of course, he did. The narcissist will tell you that you are paranoid, overly sensitive, and dramatic. After being exposed to a narcissist, you very well could be which is understandable because that was the narcissist's goal all along. Seek help from a specialist for narcissistic abuse.

Insecure – The narcissist has the lowest form of insecurity. The narcissist uses your insecurities to destroy you, belittle you, demean you, make you feel inferior, and have control over you.

Insinuate – Both the overt and the covert narcissist will insinuation tactics to manipulate you, confuse you, threaten you, bully you, and/or gaslight you. An abusive person won't necessarily come right out and tell you things you need to know; he will "insinuate" things. Insinuating gives power over information. Insinuating makes for confusion—and deciphering. You are supposed to decipher the meaning the narcissist wants you to know. There's no way to get it (the insinuated meaning) correct. You will usually always be wrong. Being "wrong" in your interpretation allows the narcissist to show disgust from the narcissist toward your "stupidity." Being "wrong" in your interpretation also allows the narcissist to gain that superiority, narcissistic fix, and control.

Instigate – The narcissist will create arguments, fights, belittling, rages to get a reaction from you. Don't fall for this trick. His righteous anger is a trap. This is the bait and bash tactic. He enjoys watching you get flustered, and maybe even flip out. He relishes this as he screams at you telling you what a wreck you are. This is how he gets his narcissistic fix.

Insulting – The narcissist is downright disrespectful and verbally abusive. The overt narcissist will insult you to your face, in private, or in front of others. This could be done as a "joke" or as an attempt to put you in your place. The narcissist's insults could be covert, passive-aggressively done in the form of "helping you to improve" by providing you with lots of negative comments. This could be done by giving positive attention to everyone else and overlooking you. It is extremely hurtful. You need to leave this relationship. Regardless of how it is done, it IS being done and it will not stop. The narcissist is an immature, jealous being who lacks being happy for others. This is a toxic person you do not want or need in your life. Get out of the relationship and surround yourself with people who are awesome and will lift you up and appreciate you.

Intense – The relationship with the narcissist is intense, especially at first. It is fast intimacy. It is fast connection building. It is intense. It is also an illusion. The narcissist is gathering information to use against you later. There will be cycles of closeness, love bombing, a connection like you have never experienced previously. You will think he is your soulmate. Then you will be blindsided by the intense bizarre crazymaking punishments, vanishing, and seeking out other partners. Be cautious when you have this intense soulmate feeling right away. Slow down. Do not allow this person to break your boundaries. Breaking your boundaries is a huge red flag. Your boundaries are in place for a reason.

Intentional – Nothing involving the narcissist against you is a mistake. It is done with purpose and on purpose. There is an agenda and the meanness is intentional.

Intentions – The purpose of the narcissist is to manipulate you, control you, and destroy you. This is done because of the extreme low self-esteem and extreme low self-worth of the narcissist. Do not try to fix the narcissist: you can't. It will be another game for the narcissist. It is a game that you will lose.

Internal dialog – The narcissist has a very negative internal dialog running in his mind. The monkey mind is running the show. He has this negative self-importance which gives him a false sense of superiority. He is self-loathing. He is also making up negative internal stories about you, as well as most everyone else around him: at work, at home, friends, and family. No one is immune to his negative internal dialog.

Interpretation – The narcissist will twist, and spin, any event, situation, dialog, conversation to suit is agenda. His interpretation is the only one that matters. All others are flat out wrong. Get used to it or leave and seek help to rebuild your confidence.

Intervention – I needed an intervention to break free from the narcissist. My original choice to leave the long-term toxic abusive relationship was to end my life. It was the only way I saw an "out." It's difficult to do because the empath, or the victim, is conditioned to behave as though everything is fine. The only things that are wrong with the relationship are the victim's fault. The victim has been conditioned not to talk about even those supposed flaws and faults with others because then we are "bad," "unlovable," "worthless." The narcissist is skilled at spinning the story of abuse, mistakes, and accidents. My intervention came via my therapist, and a judge who recommended a specialist in PTSD over an hour away. They intervened and saved my life. I am forever grateful.

Intimacy – In my opinion, experience, and research, the narcissist isn't capable of a truly close, supportive, loving relationship. An intimate relationship requires a sharing of emotional wellbeing and nurturing. The narcissist wears a mask so you really don't know what he's thinking, he' conniving, or what his hidden agenda is. The narcissist will behave as if he is being emotionally intimate with you to gather information, which will eventually be used against you.

■ 2. Intimacy – The narcissist wants to know everything about you. He wants to know your thoughts, your feelings, your successes, your weaknesses, your wounds. This feels as though this guy is enamored with you. You are drawn into sharing with him because he is so open to hearing everything, is attentive, and asks questions about you. You feel "heard" like you've never felt heard before. You feel he is lulling you into a trust of mutual care. You believe all this intimacy of sharing is to build a lasting relationship. Then, the awesome intimacy you felt from him, has suddenly left you with this odd empty feeling. You may think you've done something wrong; or, said something you shouldn't have . . . or said too much. You are now in phase two—the beginning of the destroying your self-worth, self-confidence to control you. You are now being put on the defense through manipulation of worry and manipulation to instill self-doubt. Let me give you this advice: if you have shared your story, your life with a man, and he is now withdrawing from you, Sweetie, you need to withdraw from him—IMMEDIATELY. No excuses. You need to be with someone who will never pull back from you. Anyone who pulls back from you and plants self-doubt in yourself, then the decision is made by you! HE IS NOT worth it! Reclaim your power!

Intimidates – The narcissist will blindside you with confusing, made up fantasy stories, lies, blackmail, loss of financial safety, loss of personal safety, anyway that will work to the narcissist's agenda. He will hold over your head all he has done for you (real or imagined), all he "was" going to do for you (real or imagined), how you will never have anyone better than him, and how no one will ever love you because he will tell you how unworthy, and unlovable he says you are. All those unkind things he says about you are not true. There are much better, healthy, kind, compassionate men in the world who know what it means to love and who know how to love. Break up with the narcissist, heal, and be with one of the good guys. You deserve so much better.

Introspective – From my experience, the narcissist is not a self-assessing, self-analyzing creature. The narcissist is not introspective, reflective in a positive manner. The toxic individual in my life used my compassion and sensitivity in people pleasing to justify any means to the results he wanted.

Introverted narcissist (also known as a vulnerable narcissist, covert narcissist, hypersensitive narcissist, closet narcissist). See the covert narcissist description.

Intuition – When you have a feeling something isn't right, or even safe, your intuition has taken all the facts, noticed all the minute clues, feelings, and sounds/tones and analyzes these things in less than a split second. This is your intuition at work. You have intuition. LISTEN TO IT! You know the truth. Your brain and your intuition are telling you the truth. There are red flags, caution signs, and alarms bells going off in your mind—heed the subconscious inborn, built-in protection system. Don't let some sneaky toxic person destroy you or your emotional health. LISTEN to your intuition.

Invades – The narcissist will break through your boundaries. You will end up giving the narcissist your passwords, private information, and so on. The narcissist will invade your privacy. The narcissist will also hack his way into your private world. The narcissist objective is to control you and to dominate you. You need to change all of your passwords. Cancel your credit cards and order new ones as well. You need to have stronger boundaries.

Invasion of privacy – The narcissist will follow you, hack you, listen in on your conversations, spy on you, stalk you, lurk on your social media, and happen to show up exactly where you are, and so on. I knew this when I dated him. He explained it away by saying he wanted to "take care of me." (During the mid-80s, he snuck into my parent's home when I was alone in my room. I was on the phone with my best friend. He stood in the hallway and listened to our teen girl conversation. All the clues where there, but I didn't know them. I believed him. YOU will know better. You will RUN and don't look back!)

Invested – The narcissist is invested in and is loyal to himself, his agenda, and his wants. The narcissist is not invested in you unless there is something on his agenda he wants or needs to feel superior. Make no mistake about it, it is not you he is invested in. It is a superficial quality or tangible thing you have. Once that is destroyed, the narcissist will dump you in the harshest of fashions. You will be blindsided. You will not see it coming. You will not know what happened, or how you ended up where you are. You'll wonder why he did this to you. (I know the answer. You are a pawn in the narcissist's agenda.) You need to seek help to rebuild your self-esteem.

Invisible – If you stay with a narcissist, you will become invisible to the narcissist, to your friends and family, and even to yourself. You will lose who you are . . . who you once were. You need to seek help from a counselor or therapist to work through narcissistic abuse, perhaps even PTSD, and to regain your self-worth to become empowered.

Irrational – Most of the time, the narcissist is juggling people, many lies, and manipulations all over town (including in the workplace). It can be challenging to keep all these lies in order. When the narcissist's dam begins to break, the narcissist flips out and becomes irrational. The narcissist will use more irrational lies on top of the already crazymaking stories he has told. The narcissist will feel attacked if questioned . . . even when the questions are innocent. At his core, the narcissist is irrational. When you hear something insane, or something that sounds even slightly off, and you question it only to be faced with rage, you need to know you are dealing with a toxic human being. This is not a relationship you want to pursue. Your intuition will be telling you there is something wrong with this guy. There is! Listen to your intuition. Don't try to figure it out. Just get out!

Irrelevant – You are unimportant to the narcissist. He has someone, or maybe even several women, in the wings waiting to take your place. (Let them! If they are cheaters, they deserve each other.) The narcissist will do little things to let you know that you are irrelevant. You can't bring them up or you will appear to be petty or crazy. If you do bring them up, which the narcissist wants you to do, you will be belittled. The narcissist will do this with big things as well – blatantly in your face, there's no other way to look at it. Should you bring this up to the narcissist, you will be belittled and made a fool. You are irrelevant. Leave this relationship.

Irresponsible – The narcissist may seem like he has it all together and is well balanced. Below the surface, this guy is a mess. There are areas within himself he has absolute control. There are other areas, addictions, he cannot control. The additions are where you can see where the narcissist is irresponsible. The narcissist may seem unreliable, saying he will meet you, and then forgets. The narcissist is not being an airhead in forgetting to meet you, pick up something or someone for you, the narcissist simply does not care about you. He is purpose-fully thoughtless in relation to you.

Irritable – After the romance, "soulmate" portion begins to fade, you will experience more and more irritability from the narcissist. This is to make you feel worried, fill yourself with self-doubt, and manipulate you. If someone if irritable, that's on them, not you. You cannot cause another person to treat you poorly. They make that decision. Your decision must be to go no contact from this toxic person.

Isolates – The narcissist wants to remove you from your emotionally healthy friends, family, and workmates. The abuser wants to create distance between you and your support network and your resources. (He will tell you he is the only one who has your back. Meanwhile, he is destroying you emotionally, financially, mentally, and so on.) The abuser will separate you from support and resources by bullying you, harassing you, making you feel worthless, shame, and guilt for having these people in your life. The abuser will likely escalate to not giving you access to your finances, autos, banking records, tax information, cell phone. My advice to you: No one needs to tell you who you can and cannot have as family, friends, or even workmates especially when these people are emotionally healthy. The narcissist is afraid of them. The narcissist is afraid of being exposed, which is why he wants to isolate you from the supportive, good people in your life.

J

Jaded – The narcissist will tell you outright how jaded he is, but only you understand him. He will tell you that you are the only person in which he can confide, and trust. Only you. Only . . . that is a lie. He's given his lines to other compassionate, empathetic women to snare his targets into his web. He thinks we are all stupid, falling for his stories. (Are his stories real or made up? Who knows and quite frankly, who cares). He will tell you his stories of past relationships who maligned him (and there could be many). He will share tales of his abusive, or sad childhood and all that he had to endure to bring out your maternal caring instincts. Beware. While the narcissist is clever . . . and maniacal, he is not original. He uses this "only girl in the world" who understands his strategy on all his targets. If it works with one, he will use it on others (maybe with some modification).

Jealous – The narcissist is envious of everyone, regardless of the narcissist's own position or place in life. During love bombing, the narcissist will use the excuse that the jealous behavior is because he loves you so much. Or perhaps, he tells you his jealousy is not jealousy at all but a protective measure because you clearly do not have the brains to see when someone is/is not a threat to you. The narcissist is jealous of everyone and considers most everyone to be a threat. The narcissist does not trust anyone . . . not even himself. Because the narcissist is in a victim mentality, the narcissist cannot be happy for anyone or for their success. (Even if the success is that of his own child.) The jealousy is a trait of a developmentally immature person. You deserve to be with a person of worth, standards, and maturity.

Jekyll/Hide – The narcissist can flip emotional states so quickly. He can be calm and seemingly engaged in a conversation or television show (something generic). The next moment he has become enraged, seething with anger over nonissues. He will twist and turn things around in his mind and will lash out at you. Whatever it is, he will blame you for it. He will escalate into a bossy person, to mean, to gaslighting, to baiting and bashing, and an all-out rage at you. Over what though? Who knows. It is his issue that he has projected onto you. Leave. Leave now. It will never get better. (He might even tell you that during his rage. BELIEVE HIM!)

Jerk – Name-calling is not appropriate. Do not lower yourself to the narcissist's level while he baits you, pokes and prods you to do so. You will think in your mind, "what a jerk!" (And you are right!) If your intuition is telling you this person is not the one for you, listen to it! Move on (regardless of his sad sack story the narcissist will use to attempt to evoke pity and give a reason for the bad behavior.) There are better fish in the sea.

Jokes – The narcissist will give you put-downs, and will disparage you in the form of "jokes." (Oh, he is just so funny, is he? And it's at your expense. He's a jerk.) You will feel off-balanced when he does this. You know you want to say something about it; but if you do you will be chastised by him. He will declare how you cannot take a joke and he will be sure not to joke around with you anymore. (Is that an insinuation that he will "joke" with others . . . that he will cheat on you? The answer is "yes, yes it is.) He is not worth your time because you are awesome.

Juggles – The narcissist will have a harem of others in which he juggles. Chances are when the narcissist is giving you the silent treatment, has withdrawn affection from you, and is breadcrumbing you, he is with someone else or several other people. Do not compete for the narcissist's attention (that's what he wants you to do). Do not hope he "picks you" once again. Once the narcissist has given you the silent treatment or has withdrawn affection from you, you go no contact. Do not reply to him at all. There is nothing positive that will come from it, even if he "comes back" to you. This will be temporary. It will not last. Go no contact.

Justification – The narcissist will righteously defend and justify his lies, manipulations, crazymaking, and so on usually with more blatant outrageous lies, or will blameshift, gaslight, and project whatever it is onto you. The narcissist always has a reason. One of the reasons is to justify why he hurt you. He will make up a story to justify his awful behavior toward you (which is also turning the tables on you, blame shifting, and giving you the "you made me" abusive reasoning. If the narcissist does not have a reason, he will create a fantasy story lie and stick with that to justify his inappropriate toxic behavior. Beware—he just might turn the tables on you and use you as his justification.

K

Karma – Let karma do its work as you close the door on this relationship. You will not get closure. You must trust that karma, the universe, God, or whatever your Higher Power is, is working for you. Seek help to get over him, to improve your self-worth, and confidence. One of the best ways to let karma work for you is to simply forgive and release the negative feelings. It is not easy, so surround yourself with the best, most supportive people to hold your hand or give you a shoulder to cry on during the healing process. You will, I promise, make it through to the other side. (The other side is glorious!)

Kindness – You have heard someone say, "Do not mistake my kindness with weakness." Well, the narcissist exploits your kindness. He does use your kindness and weakness. The narcissist will do it again and again and again.

Know-it-all – You may be a specialist in your industry, and graduated at the top of your class. The narcissist still knows more than you. (And, isn't afraid to "put you in your place.") While you may be making headway in your career, the narcissist is jealous of you. The narcissist will undermine your efforts, belittle you, and make fun of you either outright and perhaps aggressively, or covertly as a joke or under the narcissist's breath. You don't need to be with someone who is not supportive of you and undermines you with unkind remarks.

L

Lacks reliability – After the love bombing stage, a time when the narcissist appears to give you attention, and appears to make plans with you, the next stage is filled with confusion and lack of reliability to honor commitments and often plays a shell game with plans—adding in choices and changing the plans on a whim, followed by blaming you for not knowing what is going on, or claiming he told you, claiming you told him something different. His lack of reliability will make you question yourself. Don't fall victim to this game. You cannot and will not win. The only way to be safe is to not make plans with him at all . . . and do not wait by the phone for him to call because he won't until it's "too late" to do the activity you were hoping to do and will engage you in an argument over it.

Language – The language the narcissist uses is purposeful. It is meant to belittle you, harm you, and hurt you. You will be told you are "too sensitive" or "you misunderstood" or "why can't you let it go?" It is meant to make you question yourself and to throw you off balance. Trust me, you heard correctly; you're not too sensitive, and you would love to let it go if only he would stop blaming you. When you begin self-questioning after an interaction with the narcissist who throws you off balance, do this: go no contact immediately! You do not owe the narcissist an explanation. The narcissist will only use it against you.

Lashes out – The narcissist will lash out unexpectedly and will blindside you. The narcissist's rage is huge and will be directed at you for the most trivial of things. Things that you may or may not even be aware of. You may be walking with the narcissist in a conversation with the narcissist and suddenly you feel an energy change. There may be a silent treatment that you do or do not notice (depending on how deep you are into talking), but a rage will occur out of the blue. Take note of where you are for your safety. Do not engage or try to defend yourself verbally against the narcissist's nonsensical temper tantrum. There is no reasoning with a narcissist. Once you are home, or in a place of safety, go no contact from this abuser. Seek help from a specialist to improve your self-worth.

Laughter – Forget about authentic laughter. You may notice you do not laugh as much together after the love bombing stage has ended. You may notice you do not laugh much at all. Your happiness and joy will be replaced by worry and sadness. The narcissist will throw some breadcrumbs your way every now and then to control you. The happiness laughter is short-lived, and not real. The narcissist is not interested in seeing you happy or having joy.

Layered – Your emotional wounds are layered and deep. The narcissist used emotional warfare on your unsuspecting psyche. You will need help healing from the pain and wounds created by the narcissist.

Lazy – The narcissist will delegate as much as possible . . . and, will take positive credit for everything. The narcissist is a whiner and is lazy; unless there is an opportunity for him to "save the day." He will do something in the short term to gain attention and praise. The narcissist enjoys the appearance of being the one who "saves the day" because "without him" nothing is possible.

Learned helplessness – You will begin to feel incapable of being able to do anything including making decisions, finances, choosing a car, selecting an outfit, planning a trip, picking a restaurant. The narcissist has groomed and conditioned you to become emotionally helpless and insecure. The narcissist wants you to be dependent only on him so he can control you. You must seek help from an expert or specialist in recovering from narcissistic abuse syndrome.

Let them walk – Anyone who does not want to be in your life, do not chase after them. If someone leaves you or walks out of your life for any reason: let them walk! Better people who will elevate you will appear for you. This includes friends, family, coworkers, and anyone who walks out when you need support and compassion.

Lies – Lies are almost a special language for the narcissist. The narcissist will look you straight in the eye and lie to you. As you're in a slight pause, trying to make sense of what was said it you (because you don't believe it but are trying to make it truth), the narcissist generally interjects the pause with something to throw off your thought process with more dialog, or single words ("what? What?") If you follow up with more questions, the narcissist will make you seem as though you are causing drama; or worse. The narcissist will become enraged. The narcissist uses lies for most everything and will lie about most everything even the most innocuous and harmless of topics. If you ask a question, one in which you know the answer, you will receive a lie or a confusing response. You cannot trust the words a narcissist says. Do not try. Do not attempt to reason with this person. Do not try to rationalize or decipher the narcissist. The narcissist is lying to you because the narcissist does not have respect for you . . . at all. None. Leave this relationship to heal and improve your life not worrying if someone is lying to you anymore.

Lionize – The narcissist will treat you like the only girl in the world. The narcissist will treat you like you are special, the most important person. This is all a farce. It is an illusion. Once the narcissist has you under his control, you will be treated like the opposite. You will be treated like dirt.

Listen for the clues – The narcissist will tell you many tales of how he was screwed over by his last wife (wives), all most all the girlfriends in his past. He will tell you stories about all of them. Here's the thing: ALL of them? Seriously? That's the clue. Truth be told: HE is the problem. Listen closely to all his stories of how these past relationships "hurt" him or he was "the victim" or how he was wronged in some manner because he will be telling the same story about you to his next one.

Listen to your intuition – Your intuition has been telling you all along that this guy is toxic. The narcissist has been playing havoc with your emotions making you feel inferior. You are not inferior. Do not believe him or his innuendoes. When you finally acknowledge your intuition, you need to seek help from an expert or specialist in rebuilding after narcissistic abuse.

Listeners – At first, you and this person will spend seemingly endless amounts of time texting, emailing, talking on the phone and being together. This person seems to hang on your every word. You will things this person is such a good listener and is attentive. He's not. He's learning what makes you tick. He's figuring out your strengths and weaknesses. You have shared your personal secrets, hopes, dreams, and fears. Boom. He has you in what you think is an exclusive relationship. Now, without warning, he will use those things against you to serve his own sick agenda. His agenda is one of aggression and hostility to shred you to pieces. He does not love you. He never has. He never will.

Live – The narcissist expects you to live your life for him. He expects you to like all that he likes. He expects you to do all that he wants. STOP IT! It's one thing to be lovingly helpful and supportive in someone's pursuits, it's quite another when it is demanded and expected of you. When you find yourself canceling your plans, changing your life and lifestyle to be the narcissist's lackey to the point where your own pursuits begin to suffer, become less important, or become nonexistent, it is time to acknowledge to yourself that you are in a relationship with a narcissist. You must go no contact from your narcissist so that you can take your life back, and become empowered. (Narcissists hate to see their victims begin to get self-confidence back and become empowered as much as they hate you going no contact.)

Lives in the past – You are likely to hear stories of the narcissist's glory days that occurred ten, twenty, thirty or forty years ago during junior or senior high school. That is because the narcissist is stuck in that developmental period. A narcissist might send you pictures of himself . . . from that period of his life. Recounting tales of junior high, high school, the bus, the music, and the fashions. It's all about that time. He snares you with his "reminiscing." I don't call it reminiscing. I call it being stuck in the past. He's not that age, even if he thinks he is and speaks as though these things just happened. They haven't.

Lizard brain – The lizard brain is the oldest part of our brains. It gives us the primitive signals of fight or flight. You will notice many of the narcissist's actions line up with the lizard brain. The narcissist is in a constant fight, turmoil, or flight/fleeing from something. When you notice the lizard brain reactions, you must notice that the narcissist is unable to truly emotionally bond with someone. The lizard brain is in fight or flight. It destroys or runs away. You will see the narcissist doing this constantly. It is exhausting.

Logic – When dealing with a narcissist, there is no logic in following the narcissist's thought process. You will try to make sense of issues, but that makes it worse for you. This gives the toxic person the opportunity to open up some crazymaking, and gaslighting tactics on you. Your logic may be on point; but, the abuser will twist everything you say around—turning the tables on you. He may even take it to the point where he says what you are saying "never happened" or not in the way you "imagined" it happened. (That's a favorite stunt of the abuser.) Changing events, denying them and conversations, turning the tables on you to make you feel undermined, confused, and so on is meant to chip away at your –self-worth. If this has become a pattern that you've realized, you need to leave this relationship because it is not going to get any better.

Logical fallacy – The narcissist will use "valid" but untrue statements against you to further his cause. Valid but untrue means it is a lie or untrue for you and your circumstances. The narcissist is twisting something around. These are manipulations to throw you off balance and confuse you. It is deceptive. It is superficial. He has no real basis to chastise you so he pulls things out of the air. Leave this jerk. You deserve better.

Lonely – You will feel alone while you are in a relationship with a narcissist, even if the narcissist is sitting right there beside you. When the narcissist is not with you, you will feel all lone . . . very lonely. Guess who isn't ever alone. The narcissist! He has a stable of "others" from which to get his pathetic attention.

Loner – The narcissist will claim he's a loner. It's a bent truth (aka—a lie). The narcissist has a stable of partners. If the narcissist is a loner, it is because no one likes him anymore after all his narcissistic antics.

Love – The narcissist does not love you. The narcissist has never loved you. The narcissist has never loved anyone. You will be compared to others, but the narcissist did not love them either. The narcissist does not know how to give love or receive love. The narcissist will "take" your love. Love is an unknown, unrealistic concept to the narcissist. The narcissist may be so bold as to tell you he does not know how to love. This is true. You may think you will be the one who reaches his heart. The truth is YOU WILL NOT BE LOVED by a narcissist. Your narcissist may even be so bold as to admit to you that he has never loved you in the first place. This is done to see how deep you are under his control, how much self-esteem you have lost. Your happiness is worth so much more than you are giving it credit. You will have an aching pain to want to rekindle the relationship you had in the beginning, and wonder, "where did he go?" Or you will wonder, "how can I make this right?" because you have been blamed yet again. You must know this: the "real" persona the narcissist was showing you at first, while love bombing you, was a made-up, fake, false persona. That person never existed. That person was created based on your blueprint the narcissist stole from you to give you the illusion he was your perfect other half, your "soulmate." It's a lie. It's all a lie. The narcissist is a user and only wants you to prove something to himself. You were a challenge. The narcissist snatched you away from your life, leading you on with lies, promises, and fantasies of a future with him. It is never going to happen. It's time to leave this loveless person. You cannot change or help this person. His heart is black. You need to seek help in learning to love yourself, building yourself back up, finding your true passion, and your empowerment. He does not love you. He will never love you. (He will not love the next one either so dismiss that from your mind.)

Love bombing – This is the first step in the narcissist's bag of manipulative tricks. The narcissist will make you feel special, like a soulmate, like there is no one else like you in the world and he's been searching for you his entire life. This short period of time is when the narcissist shows you attention, texts you, emails you, communicates with you in a supportive, attentive, loving, interested manner. The narcissist may refer to you for decisions and ask for your help with something seemingly important to make you feel honored. IT'S AN ILLUSION. If you feel this awesome, intoxicating feeling fast and at first, be very wary, be very cautious. This is love bombing. It's a tactic used by the narcissist. This is when victims get drawn into the narcissist's web of lies, deceit, and illusion. As soon as the love bombing turns from the extreme valuing of you, the narcissist will begin to devalue you. As soon as you feel that uncomfortable, "that's not what I meant" feeling . . . turn and run! Let the narcissist think whatever it is he wants to think about you. Go no contact from the narcissist.

Love triangle – The narcissist wants to believe he is super special, above all others, is highly prized and sought after in various aspects including partners. A narcissist collects sexual partners while he is in a "relationship" with you. A narcissist loves the competition for his affection. The narcissist enjoys watching partners humiliate themselves to be chosen . . . to be picked. The narcissist bounces between the partners. The narcissist does not care if you know. There's fun in hiding it; but if you find out, there is a new level of challenging in seeing if he can make you believe his lies. A committed relationship doesn't exist when you are with a narcissist; although you are expected to be faithful and loyal. The narcissist is not faithful. Marriage doesn't matter. Rules of decency and society don't apply to the narcissist . . . just to everyone else. The narcissist is above those and believes he can get away with just about anything. Seek help in improving your self-esteem. The narcissist has destroyed it. You deserve better. Get out now before you get a disease.

Low self-esteem – Low self-esteem is too evolved for the narcissist's personality description. The narcissist's self-esteem is extremely poor and he is deeply insecure. His self-esteem is so low he cannot ever be happy for anyone else because of his own self-hatred. With all that said, they put out a calm, confident demeanor. It is an illusion. The narcissist put out an overly confident self-esteem: he gets what he wants. He is unemotional about it. The only thing a narcissist is passionate about is himself, his likes, his needs, his goals, his desires, and especially his agenda. The narcissist hides his insecurities by being overly confident, obnoxious, ruthless, by being a victim, and by just plain cruel.

Loyalty – The narcissist expects and demands complete and total loyalty regarding all topics and issues. If you have your own opinion, which is different from the narcissist, you are inferior, wrong, disloyal, and the enemy. There may be things you think show loyalty to you by the narcissist, but don't be fooled. The narcissist is using you to mask who he is, or for in some way to further his agenda. The narcissist is loyal only to himself. The narcissist is loyal only to himself. The narcissist is loyal only to himself.

Lures – The narcissist pays attention to you, a lot of attention to you. The narcissist during love bombing will pay for things, treat you special, and buy you cards, and flowers, and gifts. The narcissist asks you questions finding out about your strengths and weaknesses, achievements, hopes, and dreams. The narcissist confides in you about stories of woe and how no one has ever understood him like you. You are the only one he trusts. You are the only one he feels connected . . . until he connects with someone else. You will feel like the only girl in the world to him (he might even use the song by Rihanna as his ringtone for you, and his side chick, and some other chick, oh and another side, side chick too). The narcissist will love bomb you; then, will find a reason to get mad at you.

M

Maladaptive behaviors – Watch, just watch. You'll see. If you think he's a narcissist, the rude, toxic behaviors will surface. In society, we have adaptive behaviors to get along and live peacefully with each other. The narcissist is either overtly or covertly creating havoc on other's lives. While the narcissist is not running around like a wild animal attacking people; the narcissist is emotionally draining people of positivity to make them feel inferior and worthless. It's not just you. The narcissist has contempt for most everyone.

Malicious – The intentions of the narcissist are evil and self-serving. What can the narcissist really do to hurt you? Create havoc on your emotional stability, call you names, emotionally and verbally abuse you, financially abuse you, sexually abuse and/or exploit you, humiliate you, and will spread hurtful lies about you. The narcissist is completely and totally spiteful. The narcissist WILL call you spiteful. Don't fall for that narcissist's blame shifting. (Seriously, do you really think this guy is your soulmate and destiny? He is going to destroy you.)

Malignant – The narcissist is always looking for negativity and spiteful outcomes that infect those around him.

Manipulates – The word "manipulates" is not a strong enough word to describe the destruction of your personality, and emotional wellbeing, as well as emotional strength. The narcissist finds the piece you are weak at and uses this as his entry point to infect your worthiness and security. Your intuition will tell you that "something" isn't right. Listen to your intuition!

Martyr – While the narcissist is "the best" at everything, he is also the tops at all types of suffering. As with other negative manipulations the narcissist amps up, the narcissist increases his suffering to epic proportions. After all, the narcissist martyr is will say he's with you . . . the one who holds him back, the one who causes him to suffer. The narcissist martyr is there only for you, to take care of you because without the toxic narcissist, you are nothing and would fail . . . even die. The narcissist will claim he is this caregiver of yours because you are incapable of taking care of yourself. (Well, if you have been with this toxic person long enough, and he has undermined and destroyed all your self-worth, including decision making, you might feel like that. It may take time to recover and get back on your feet. That's okay. Take your time. You've been through hell and back at the expense of "the martyr."

Mask – The narcissist wears a disguise when you first meet. The narcissist seems charming, awesome, wants to spend all his time with you, is your "soul mate" . . . or makes you believe he is your soul mate—your perfect, ideal partner. He's not. He tricked you. He manipulated you. Once the mask comes off, you never will see that awesome person again because it wasn't real, legitimate, or sincere. It was a game of control and domination.

Measuring up – The narcissist holds himself in high esteem. It is you he wants to compare with others to tear you down and diminish your successes and personal self-worth. You won't measure up to the narcissist's ever-changing and twisted expectations. Stop trying. Stop crying. And just get off the crazy train.

Medical issues – As with all professional sufferers from maladies, the narcissist is plagued with many and varied medical issues. The narcissist's medical issues are never-ending.

Megalomania – At the extreme end of the sliding scale, the narcissist has a belief that he is supremely powerful, intelligent, and clever. (Even the CEO must report to someone. There is no "supremely" powerful person.) This power is in business, in finances, in the home, in school, in entertainment, in social situations, in sports, and so on. Power is a major component in the narcissist's being. This is also called delusions of grandeur. The narcissist thinks he is the most relevant and superior person in the room. He may not show it overtly to others, but he will make sure you know it, and that you respect it.

Menace – The narcissist is a menace to himself, and that is his problem. It's not yours to fix. The narcissist is a menace to others. That is where you come in. You need to step out of denial mode, self-questioning, and doubt mode. It is what it is. He is toxic. Get out of the toxic environment to seek help and heal.

Mental disorder – Narcissism is a diagnosed psychological problem. Only a trained medical professional can help the narcissist work through issues.

Microaggressions – These are the tiny, slightest of slight, passive-aggressive as well as outright aggressive, actions, behaviors, statements that are designed to make you feel inferior and undermine your self-worth, question your own judgment, turn innocent even generic interactions into big situations, and to place in you under his control. These are the manipulative actions of a well-established toxic individual. They assist in the narcissist's gaslighting tactics to confuse you.

Mimic – The narcissist wants to gain your trust in a rapid way. He will mimic your actions, your likes, your dislikes, your style, and anything else he can. This is a manipulation. The narcissist can be a chameleon changing so easily because he doesn't have his own authentic personality. He copies others to build rapport. When you have fallen for him because you have "so much in common," don't be surprised when he dumps you. It's what he does for fun and for sport. It's how he increases his false sense of superiority.

Mind games – He will not support you. He will not console you. He does not accept any disagreement or constructive criticism. He will make fun of you. He will be snarky. He will be sarcastic. He will put you down. He will exaggerate. He will use the same abusive mind games and tactics that were used on him.

Mind reader – Do you have magic abilities to predict what it is the toxic person wants when he wants it, exactly as he wants it? You will be expected to "just know" he "needed" something, or wanted something, wanted to do something, be somewhere. You will be required to be all-knowing when it comes to his needs, wants, and desires. You will catch all sorts of belittling, character assignation, and chipping away at your self-worth in being a "bad" person as well as an unfit partner. (But don't worry, he will forgive you after his flip out and will give you another chance to get it right.) Leave this jerk. You can do better!

Mind reading – The narcissist believes he knows what it is you are thinking, what you've done, what you "meant" and interprets these things in such a manner that he believes he knows your divisive, sneaky ulterior motives. (The toxic person always thinks you have ulterior motives. Why does he, then stay with you, the one he believes has ulterior motives? He simply wants to control you and make you dependent on him.) He believes he is cleverer than you and you cannot hide your evil doings from him. When in fact, you have done nothing wrong. The narcissist can and will spin anything to suit his needs, to throw you under the bus. Listen to what it is he is saying when he is doing his interpreting. When he does his interpreting of you, he is telling you what he is up to but has projected it in a twisted way to place blame on you.

Mindfulness – The narcissist is not mindful. He plays mind games.

■ The victim should practice mindfulness meditation to help with healing.

Minimizing – The narcissist will minimize your needs, desires, and struggles as unimportant because you are unimportant to the narcissist. The narcissist will create problems; and, then will minimize your feelings by talking down to you, belittling you, ignoring you, and even denying the situation and/or your feelings.

Mirroring – The narcissist mirrors you when you are first together to gain your trust. It's a trick. Once I tried "mirroring" my abuser to show him what I saw, to show him how he was treating me. It backfired big time. It turned into opportunities for him to bait and bash me and to make me feel bad. There is no repairing the toxic person by a partner. The narcissist needs long-term medical treatment. You aren't it.

Miscommunicates – If you pick up on the narcissistic changing the rules often, and you are often "getting it wrong" it is because the narcissist is purposefully vague, and purposefully miscommunicates. It is a tactic to throw you off balance. He uses it to start arguments as well. You will be blamed for all miscommunication.

Misinterpret – You will be accused of not understanding something correctly. You misunderstood. You interpreted the scenario incorrectly. You will be gaslighted and blamed for the incorrect analysis of the scenario, discussion, plans, message, or whatever. For example, when you walk into your husband's office and his latest is leaning up against, or sitting in, in his space—right out in the open—your intuition is to turn around, but you continue forward. When it is brought up, the narcissist will lie right to your face telling you that you did not see what you saw. YOU misunderstood. YOU misinterpreted the events. (When he leaves you for her, you will know you did not "get it wrong." That event, and your willingness to accept what he lays on you as guilt will cause you nightmares.) Get out now. If you are married, get a divorce attorney immediately. Trust me, you need one. (He already has one lined up; along with an apartment with his new person, a new bank account, and so on. Oh, he is ready. He was ready long ago. Ask me how I know. My former husband played this strategic mind game with me. Pretending we were happily married—and all that goes with it. He put all his ducks in a row first. Blindsiding you is a favorite game of the toxic individual.

Misrepresenting – The toxic person has totally mispresented who he is, and what his beliefs are. This is done to gain your trust.

Mistreat – If you feel mistreated, you need to leave the relationship regardless if the person is a narcissist or not. Mistreatment is mistreatment. Get out now before it escalates.

Mistress – The narcissist has one, or two, or three, or an entire stable of others from whom he can get attention and sex.

Mocking – The toxic, immature person will make fun of you and will mock you. Mocking is an immature, low-level tactic that is indicative of his emotional development. If you are being mocked, you are being mistreated. The "teasing" may be overt or covert, in an isolated setting or in front of others. The narcissist is unpredictable so there is no way to guess when it will happen.

Monkey mind – The negative chatter in your mind. It can be negative self-talk or that of the narcissist that your mind as adopted. It might be as if you hear his voice in your mind telling you awful things about yourself. The monkey mind is a terrible experience. You must get help learning to quiet the monkey mind and taking back your self-worth. Step one is to go no contact from your narcissist.

Monster – The narcissist is a toxic monster. The overt narcissist is a more obvious monster. The covert narcissist is a sneaky snake monster. Get out of this relationship. Seek help for abuse.

Mood swings – The narcissist's mood swings are legendary. He can flip on a dime, and in an instant. He is unpredictable. He can be explosive or will show mild annoyance directed at you. You most certainly are the target.

Moody – The narcissist seems to be in a constant aggravated or moody state. You will jump through hoops trying to please him or make him happy. Forget about him, and learn to make yourself happy. Your inner peace depends on it.

More – It is never enough with the narcissist. You give him all you can, and it is still not enough, not good enough. You will most likely hear your inner voice tell you this. LISTEN TO IT! You might even hear the narcissist tell you this in one of several ways. The narcissist may outright tell you what you gave him wasn't enough/good enough. The narcissist may tell you that YOU need too much in a derogatory manner. That is one of the projection tactics. The narcissist is telling you what he wants. Be on the alert because narcissist's need for "more" of whatever he wants is insatiable.

Motive questions – The narcissist will ask you pointed questions to blindside you and throw you off balance during a conversation. These questions are twisted. They may not even relate to the topic at hand. He is attempting to deflect you from whatever he has done, his responsibility, his behavior, or because he is "losing." It is always a competition—a competition where one of you will win and one of you will lose. This is how the narcissist wants it. The relationship from the narcissist's point of view will always be a "me versus you" one. You are not on the same side. This is not a balanced relationship.

Moving on – So you've decided to go no contact (hooray for you). Brace yourself. If you made the decision, either during one of the narcissist's ghosting/dumping exercises, or you've finally had enough and are ready get off the crazy train, you need to be prepared for all sorts of hell to rain down on your head by the narcissist because "how DARE you leave HIM!" He will slander you, send out the flying monkeys, stalk you, eavesdrop, spy on you, make promises of change, fly into rages, will bait and provoke you to bash you later with his "proof" that "you" are the narcissist or the unstable partner. (It will happen. It is okay; don't beat yourself up over it. The narcissist is slick and manipulative. You are no match for him.) The narcissist will do whatever he wants or needs to do to provoke a reaction from you . . . to open that proverbial door to communication. Don't fall for it. He has not changed. He does not love you. You are nothing to him. He has others—let him have at them. In the meantime, you strengthen your self-worth. Most likely you will need help from a specialist to do this.

N

Name calling – The immature developmental level will have the narcissist calling you names, making fun of you, mocking you. Instead of talking, or having a civil conversation with you, he will use the most immature, childish tactics. The narcissist will call you names when he is in a discussion, argument, or conversation with you when you fail to agree with him. If he has done something unkind or wrong and you bring it up, you will be belittled and most likely you will be called names. This is done because the narcissist is emotionally stunted and extremely immature, regardless of education level. The narcissist's goal is to make you feel inferior at any costs. The narcissist is unable to follow through with rational conversations without resorting to childish behavior. The narcissist will especially employ this tactic when he perceives he is losing the conversation, argument, situation, or even board game. This will not change. If someone calls you a name, get out of this relationship because it will happen again, again, and again. Being called a name is not an isolated incident.

Narrative – The narcissist will change the meaning of most anything he chooses. He wants to control the direction of the conversation and the story. He will straight up lie to change the facts of the situation. His flying monkeys will eat up anything he throws to them. He enjoys the drama too.

Needs, needs, needs – Oh dear God, there are so many needs. He will whine, complain, pout, use childish tactics, and manipulate you to fulfilling his needs. He will compare all his issues to yours to prove to you why he is more worthy of "needing" over your contrasting need (or needs). His needs are always more self-righteously more important and devastating than yours could ever possibly be.

■ Needs MORE of whatever the narcissist can take from you!

Needs constant adoration – If the narcissist does not receive constant praise, gratitude, thanks, notice, or adoration, you will be punished. This could come in the form of yelling, an argument, or the silent treatment and vanish or run away. You better learn your lesson or else he will increase his punishments against you. I would advise that you block him when he does his punishment. There is no reason in the world to treat you this way over his constant need for adoration and praise. What a jerk. Get out now.

Needy – The narcissist will call you needy. This is what he has created in you through his manipulative narcissistic abuse. You can stop this by going no contact from the narcissist and his narcissistic abuse. You are stronger than you realize. You can be empowered against the need to feel needy.

Negative – To say that the narcissist "is negative" is not a strong enough description. The narcissist lives in a world of negativity. He is trying to drag you down into it. Don't go. Be a positive person and surround yourself with positive people. Let him go to one of the other women he has in his stable to be negative.

Neglect – The narcissist will find a reason to be away from you. The narcissist will find a reason to create an argument so he can be away from you so he can go running around. He can later blame you for the argument and blame you for his cheating. You "made" him cheat, after all. (That is one of the narcissist's favorite lines: "You made me . . .") The narcissist will use the silent treatment on you as a punishment. Perhaps you did not give him enough attention while you were pursuing a new niche, charity work, volunteerism, or something philanthropic and good for society. He will ruin you, your reputation, embarrass you, and will leave you for a married coworker. (Oh wait, that happened to me. Let it be known, though, he will punish you in some way.)

Neglectful – The narcissist will neglect to do things for you that you were counting on. Of course, it is your fault. The narcissist will find a way to blame you for his actions. You were once his number one. He made you feel that you were his most important person. Now you are last on his list. The frizz head girl in the cube two over from him is even more important than you.

Neurotic – From my experiences, the narcissist is unbalanced and unstable. This could manifest in illnesses, headaches, migraines, never-ending searches for diagnoses, control, finances, work, cleanliness, and so on, to an extreme point.

Never ending – If you remain in the relationship with a narcissist, the abuse, the drama, the put-downs will be never-ending. The blame shifting, the lies, the cheating, the bizarre behavior will be never-ending. It does not get better. If you think it is bad now, then you have no idea how much worse it will get. Get out now!

Nice guy syndrome – It is a real thing, and it's not nice at all. You are close to this "nice guy." You think he is perfect . . . like the boy next door type of fantasy perfect. He's nice in every way. He is a saint. Things are going great. Then there is something and perhaps it bothered you. Naturally, you want to mention it so he knows how you feel/felt. So you tell him. UH OH! You just flipped the switch! The toxic gaslighting, projecting, bait and bash monster is exposed. Is he a narcissist? Maybe. Is he a jerk? Yes.

Nitpicking – If the narcissist can micromanage something related to you or your situation to criticize you and make you feel bad, the narcissist is going to do it. The narcissist enjoys finding faults, pointing them out and creating shame in your mind. You need to leave this relationship and seek help from a specialist.

No – The narcissist does not hear the word "no." He does not care that you do/do not want to do something. Eh. Not his problem. (The narcissist does not love you.)

No contact – No contact means you do not contact the narcissist for any reason whatsoever. You do not find a reason. You do not need to remind the narcissist of anything regarding your children (he's a grown man for heaven's sake), your life, or his life. He will attempt to get your attention in any way. You do not send a card for a funeral, for a birthday, for a death, for anything. You do not honor the concert tickets he bought for you. You do not honor the vacation you two were going to take together . . . even if you paid for it. No. No contact is no contact. At all. For any reason. You do not answer the questions the narcissist has. That is an attempt to bring you back under his fold, under his control. The narcissist will exploit that question and will exploit you. No contact means no contact. Do not tell your narcissist you are going no contact to heal. No contact means you just do it. You explain nothing to the narcissist. (He will figure it out. After all the narcissist has taught you he has a superior mind.)

■ After you are gone, he will threaten you and will do anything to get your attention. He wants contact with you. This is a challenge to the narcissist. He wants to regain and prove he still has power and control over you—HIS power and control over you. He wants to abuse you for sport. When you leave you break off the power and control the narcissist had. Do not give it back to him.

No win situations – The narcissist will create problems. No matter how hard you try to appease him, please him, or fix his latest problem, he will find fault with every solution and may even create additional ones. There is absolutely nothing you can do to make situations turn out differently because this chaos is not your fault. He is going to ruin weekends, special events, holidays, and vacations. It is what he does.

Non-apology – The only type of "apology" the narcissist will offer is the non-apology. This once again removes the blame from the narcissist and places it squarely on you or someone else. It is no apology whatsoever. It's insincere and disingenuous. It's a manipulation and a deflection.

Notorious – A narcissist is typically well known for boosting his belief that he is smarter, cleverer than everyone else. The nice guy, the covert narcissist is well known for being the calm one in the relationship as he gaslights you into looking out of control and a disaster. The narcissist generally presents himself very well in public and with people he wishes to fool or manipulate. Internally the narcissist is discrediting and thinking poorly of those even he wants to impress; because, after all, if these others were so smart, the narcissist would not be able to fool them. Ask any victim of narcissistic abuse and we will use the word notorious somewhere in the discussion. If you have thought this, then you need to leave this relationship in order to save yourself before it gets even worse.

Not good enough – The narcissist wants to instill a belief that you are not good enough for him, or for anyone, for your job, for your clothing, in your choice of a television show, in your music, and in all aspects of life the narcissist is able to manipulate. This will turn into shame and perhaps guilt. If you feel shame for your likes and dislikes, you need to seek help.

Nurturing – The narcissist is not nurturing. He gives the nurturing illusion during the initial pursuing of you. The attentive period from the narcissist is a short period of time. The narcissist is cold. The narcissist is like concrete. You must follow through with no contact so that you are able to nurture yourself in healing.

O

Obedient – I was raised to follow the rules and to do as I was told. Most individuals have a healthy sense of loyalty, obedience, and faith to make the choices congruent with maintaining order in their own lives and in society. The narcissist takes this to an extreme degree. He preys on obedient individuals. Obedience makes for a dream target. The narcissist uses loyalty, obedience, and faith as weaknesses on which pounce. If you are constantly questioning yourself because you haven't "proved your loyalty/obedience/faith" enough to the narcissist, let me tell you, the narcissist has implanted negative self-doubt seeds in your mind and they have taken root. Leave this toxic individual and seek help in building yourself back up. You deserve to be happy in your own skin.

Obey – A narcissist is slick. You are required to do what the narcissist wants to do, be who the narcissist wants you to be, behave as the narcissist wants you to behave. The narcissist expects you to obey him and to submit to him. The narcissist will brainwash you into thinking that your submission to him and your obedience to him is for him to help you and to guide you to good living and a better living with him. You are a person too. Do the things you want to do!

Obsessed – Through grooming and manipulation, the narcissist has implanted in you worry, anxiety, and fear. You may feel as if you are being obsessive in your thoughts and behaviors. The verdict is that you probably are, but this happened by design from the toxic individual. You are having obsessive thoughts about this guy all day and night is exactly what he wants you to have. One way to break this implanted manipulation is to realize what is happening is to seek help from an expert or specialist. Another way is to learn to meditate—either from a certified mindfulness meditation practitioner or guided meditation videos from the internet. Have no doubt that the narcissist is obsessed with controlling you. It is part of his game.

Offended – The narcissist is easily offended. The narcissist will make up reasons to be righteously offended. It's extreme. If you disagree with anything, the narcissist is offended and views it as a personal attack, which is usually followed by an argument, rage, and punishments.

Offensive – The narcissist is developmentally immature. The narcissist will use offensive jokes, and language. If the narcissist can control himself by not using swear words because it is not socially acceptable in a fundamentalist setting, the inappropriate offensive behavior will come out in other ways.

Ogle – The narcissist can drool over others while you are chastised for being pleasant with someone. The narcissist can do/say anything he wants with whomever he wants and will check out other people right in front of you. It's not only rude, it is disrespectful. He does this to belittle you so you feel self-conscious. Go not contact from the jerk.

Oh captain, my captain – Is that phrase running through your mind when the narcissist is speaking? The narcissist, like a captain on a ship or of a team, steers the way. This title, however, is a self-appointed title that he expects and commands others to obey. The narcissist steers the attention to himself, steers the conversation back to him, and steers you away from anyone who threatens to empower you.

Omnipotent – A Bible reference—Job 42:2: "I know that you can do all things and that no plan of yours can be thwarted." A toxic narcissist thinks he is powerful and can control anything, and anyone . . . like playing God. Is your partner this delusional? Or "sort of" acts this way? If so, you need to get out of the relationship and go no contact.

Omniscient – The narcissist is paranoid. He uses this paranoia to accuse you of things he thinks you are doing because of his all-knowing abilities in figuring out "your agenda." If you are being blamed repeatedly for things you have no hand in doing, get out of this toxic relationship. It is not going to get any better.

Only girl in the world – The male narcissist will make you feel like you are the only girl in the world (he might even make that song his ringtone for you); but it's all an illusion to fool you. While you are basking in the glow of your "soulmate," he is running around with a married mistress coworker. Just an FYI: each chick in his stable has a special ringtone, and not necessarily a name (or the correct name) attached to the number.

Opinionated – Both overt and covert narcissists have opinions. Your opinions need to be absolutely in line with his opinions or you will be belittled and treated in an inferior manner. Your opinions are wrong and will not matter.

Opposite world – For whatever reason, you will eventually share something you do not want to do. This reason could be serious, emotional, or not . . . whatever the reason, and it is your reason, you do not want to do something. The narcissist will pester, even harass you into doing whatever it is: going to see someone on the holiday, sabotaging your diet, going to a movie you absolutely do not want to see, attending an event you have no interest in attending, going to a restaurant you do not like. The narcissist will even challenge you on your reasons—making you feel bad about them. First, what a jerk. At the very least, this person has no respect for you or your feelings. This makes him a jerk at the very least. No one should do that to you.

■ There is more contrary opposite behavior. You may want to attend an event, see a movie, go to a restaurant, or take a class. You will notice you will not do these things. You will notice that you are doing his preferences instead (imagine that). Your preferences do not matter to the narcissist. The toxic person will find an amusing challenge in getting you to change your mind, or avoid doing the thing you want to do altogether. The narcissist will even "give you permission" to go on your own and to have fun. This may seem sincere. It is not sincere! Should you go (which means you are not fully under his control), then you will pay for it later. The narcissist will go out running around claiming you are doing your thing so he is going to go do his: meaning other people. Learn from this—learn who he is. He is mean. Get out now. Go no contact.

Oppressive – If you want to know what it is like to be held under water for a prolonged time without getting air, remain in a relationship with a narcissist. The narcissist is not interested in elevating you. The narcissist wants to keep you down. The narcissist is only concerned with elevating himself in any way he can to feel superior. This makes the narcissist happy.

Organic – You naturally gave your heart to this person. Now all these bizarre, unpleasant feelings are occurring, and unpleasant things are happening to you. Trust your natural instincts. Do not explain away the narcissist's behavior. Do not rationalize the narcissist's behavior. Do not make excuses for the narcissist's behavior. Honor your instincts! The universe is telling you this person is toxic!

Outrageous – The behavior, statements, beliefs of the narcissist can be bizarre. He may treat you badly, and say unkind things out of left field. If someone makes an honest mistake or does not know something, the narcissist's trigger in making the person feel low self-worth or inferior is activated.

Outside attention – The narcissist wants attention from la-di-da-di and everybody. Being with you is not enough. The narcissist has a stable of "others" he throws breadcrumbs to keep interested. The narcissist is in a continual loop of breadcrumbing, arguments with others, going silent and punishing, then will cycle to the next, repeat. Cycle to the next, repeat. The narcissist will also juggle you with others claiming you are suffocating the narcissist, or the narcissist needs space—which is time (days, weeks, months) in which you are unable to get a hold of this person, maybe only by the occasional text or email. That's because the narcissist is with someone else. You need to leave this relationship because you will never be enough. There will always be others.

Overconfident – It's an illusion. The narcissist acts like he knows it all and is always right. Ha! The narcissist is so lacking in confidence that he behaves in an arrogant, even mean, manner to cover up his lack of confidence. He will try to project it onto you. He will make it a personal attack. And it is a personal attack, but really, it's about him. He will share his insecurities, his mistakes, and misjudgments as if they are your insecurities, mistakes, and misjudgments when he is projecting onto you. A narcissist always gives himself away; you just have to listen.

Overreacting – Narcissists overreact. Narcissists blow things way out of proportion.

Overwhelmed – Because the narcissist is in crisis and self-imposed martyr roles most all the time, the narcissist is often (very often) overwhelmed. Ugh. Because he is overwhelmed, he neeeeeeds your assistance to "help" him. If you are unable to help him, you become the reason he has failed. You will be blamed.

Ownership – The narcissist does not accept responsibility for his negatively impacting actions. Someone else "made" him do it. Or, his childhood lacked in some way so now as an adult, he thinks he is entitled to do, behave, act, or take what he wants without regard for other's feelings or the impact it has on others, you, society. It's someone else's fault: the boss, you, a coworker, you, a relative, you, a friend, you, a stranger, or you.

P

Pain – The narcissist will cause emotional upheaval, hurt, and confusion to you in a systematic way. You won't know what happened. It will sneak up on you. You need to leave this relationship immediately. Go no contact from this spiteful person. The emotional pain and sadness may even feel like withdraw and trick you into thinking "Maybe he was not that bad. It was me." Sound the emergency alarm! This type of thought was implanted in you. He is THAT bad and THAT strategic. It was NOT you. It IS him! White knuckle through what you feel is pain, love (he does not love you), or addiction. If the pain caused by him is physical, call the police, and an ambulance. Even if you do not think you need an ambulance, call one because, trust me, you need a record of your bruises, injuries, and maybe even taken to a hospital for safety away from him.

Panic attacks – If you find yourself having more panic attacks, or the overwhelming feeling of panic, when thinking of interactions with the narcissist, it's time to seek help. Healthy, loving, supportive relationships should not and do not trigger panic, fear, and/or worry. You need to go no contact from this person immediately. My panic attacks CEASED after healing from the emotional trauma and PTSD I endured. I no longer have panic attacks! I had them for decades while I was with him. Now, I have none. If you are experiencing panic attacks: Girl, run! Run away and seek professional help! You need help to recover from the abuse.

Paradox – The narcissist appears to be complex being fun, entertaining, yet bossy and a little bit arrogant. What you will do is excuse the bad behavior for the charming things that you want to see in a person you like. The narcissist is testing boundaries and limits with you.

Paralyzed – You may feel stuck, trapped, unable to move when you are in a relationship with a narcissist. This happens because of the narcissist's lack of commitment to you, to making plans, upholding the plans, or changing the plans on a whim. He is purposefully confusing you so you are filled with anxiety. You certainly do not want to make the wrong decision which would upset him. You know that any choice you make will be wrong and that you will be blamed for your decision. It is an awful feeling. You can get help by going to a counselor, or professional. You need to share your story.

Paranoid – The narcissist is untrustworthy. The narcissist blame shifts his untrustworthiness onto his victim. The narcissist will make up pretend scenarios about the victim so that the narcissist is justified in his delusional rants. He uses his delusional, bizarre stories as proof that you are cheating, behaving badly, and committing all sorts of "sins." The unreasonable accusations force you to "defend" yourself against the crazymaking paranoia. These scenarios are used to justify searching your phone, going through your journal, reading your emails, following you, chastising you about your friends and family, insinuating terrible, mean accusations as truth. This is gaslighting you. Do not engage. Tell everyone you know what is happening to you by the narcissist. The narcissist is banking on you not telling anyone for fear of looking crazy. You will learn who is in your corner and who isn't . . . and that's okay. Let the ones who are not there for you leave you. They are not going to be helpful in your recovery. You need to surround yourself with positive, supportive people.

Paranoid abuse – Do you feel crazy paranoid and have these thoughts, "this is so not me? What has happened to me? What am I doing?" This paranoid behavior you are feeling and self-questioning is because you have been groomed to be paranoid by the toxic person. The narcissist is paranoid so he does things to make you feel paranoid too. Instead of building you up and reassuring you; the narcissist will create situations to leave you feeling paranoid. This is done on purpose. If you are feeling paranoid, leave this toxic person. You do not need to be treated this way and you deserve so much better. Seek help in empowerment and building up your self-esteem because even after you leave, there will be residual feelings of paranoia and mistrust.

Parental alienation – The narcissist may want to separate you from your friends and family if it suits his needs and agenda. The narcissist may create unpleasant situations to be a victim in front of others proving how terrible your friends and family are. The narcissist may be nice to their faces but will bash them in private—belittling them, calling their character into question, calling your character into question. The narcissist is going to do or say something to you to make you chose, feel inferior, or pull away from them. You will be put on the defensive. This is true, unless, of course, the narcissist has some of them worked into his agenda. If your family/parents contain a wound of some type, the narcissist will use them to hurt you. It's a manipulation. If your partner makes you feel bad about your friends or family for no reason or made up fantasy reasons (lies), this is someone you do not need in your life. Conversely, if your family and friends are seeing the unkind things the narcissist is doing, listen to them. They are not ganging up on you. There might truly be a problem with this person (and there is). He is toxic!

Participation – After the narcissist has roped you into this illusion, the narcissist will not participate in things that are important to you. The narcissist will degrade the activity, will attempt to make you feel bad for wanting to participate or do whatever it is you want to do.

■ Forget about conversations. The narcissist barely listens to what you are saying. The narcissist will "joke" that you blab on endlessly about unimportant things. If your topic is truly important, forget getting input from the narcissist. The narcissist will have toned you out, will blatantly not care/listen, or will use the narcissist trick of looking at you while you speak—looking at you as if you are an idiot, and will not have anything to offer or say . . . leaving you feeling even worse, and now even more questioning. This is not a partner for you. Get out of this pretend relationship (you're not in one after all.)

■ Should you want to discuss something important to your relationship, or solve a problem, the narcissist will not participate. He will ignore you. He will turn his head, watch tv, or look out the window. See, the thing is, you bore him. Everything and everyone, and their "trivial" issues bore him, and are a huge bother to him. Your issues are trivial to him because they take the focus off of him. My advice to you is to leave this jerk.

Partner – There is no such thing as being a partner with a narcissist. You are an object. The narcissist has people in his life he can control and abuse.

Passive aggressive – The toxic human being is passive aggressive. If you're seeing passive aggressive actions, you are dealing with someone who is at the very least immature and toxic. At the other end of the spectrum, the person is dangerous.

Passwords – My husband had every password of mine. This was not reciprocated to me. He told me it was to protect me in case I did something stupid on the internet. This would be the same reason I was not allowed to have his passwords or passwords for our accounts: because I might do something stupid to mess things up that would require him to "fix" it. My self-worth, low self-esteem, and dependency on him seemed logical to me. The narcissist will demand to know your passwords. It is wise to change them often. You will get "in trouble" when you change them and will be accused of doing things behind the narcissist's back that are untrue. You need to leave this relationship immediately. If you and your partner share accounts and passwords, that is a healthier relationship dynamic.

Pathological – The negative behavior will continue. It may lessen to control you, or lull you into a false sense of security; but make no mistake about it, the negative behavior will resume in an almost compulsive or obsessive manner.

Patronizing – The narcissist will mock you, belittle you, and make fun of you. The narcissist is condescending.

Pattern of behavior – If you are with the narcissist long enough, you may think you are able to pick up on a pattern of behavior. You will see extreme behavior at certain times. Other times, the toxic rages or behaviors come out of the blue. My question is why try to figure out when he is going to abuse you, humiliate you, cheat on you, and lie to you next? Instead of trying to "contain" his behavior, seek help in improving your confidence, esteem, and worth. You are truly worth so much more than putting up with any sort of abuse.

Peaceful – Narcissists can't stand peace. The narcissist creates unpleasantness on purpose. He wants your environment to be filled with worry and anxiety. The narcissist gets his narcissistic release by getting you more upset than he is. You need to not engage with a narcissist when he is taunting, blaming, picking, sabotaging you. It is him. It is not you. Remain calm and remain above it all. It is his issue, not yours.

People pleaser – Are you a people pleaser? The narcissist loves people pleasers. A people pleaser is not a challenge, so the people pleaser is an easy target. However, you're a people pleaser which means you want to please everyone, not just the narcissist. That won't do for the narcissist. The narcissist wants your allegiance and your loyalty to extreme limits. This will cause the narcissist to belittle you, the people you trust, the people you respect, and the people you love. The narcissist will attempt to isolate you from this healthy support. Don't fall for it. You hang out with whomever you want. I suggest you seek assistance in figuring out why you are a people pleaser in the first place or else you will be a doormat and vulnerable for other toxic people. You need to increase your self-worth and your self-esteem.

People pleasing – The narcissist uses your weaknesses to shame you into people pleasing him. This is also intended to diminish your power. When you people please, you are inauthentic to yourself. Don't let the narcissist steal your personality, likes, or dislikes away from you. People pleasing is not pleasing at all.

Perceptions – The only interpretation of events the narcissist will believe are the narcissist's version of events—regardless if they are true or not. The narcissist will skew the facts and reality to make them fit into his perceptions and interpretations.

Perfect – We all like things to run smoothly. The toxic narcissist takes running smoothly to new levels, including arguing about "the small stuff" that are truly insignificant. To the narcissist, nothing is insignificant. Thank heavens the narcissist is there to "save the day" by finding the flaws and pointing them out to you.

Performer – And the award for best actor in a scene is: the narcissist! Of course, the narcissist is the best actor; he fools everyone. No one knows the truth of who he really is behind that mask he is wearing. But you do. My advice to you is to get out now before it gets worse.

Permission – The narcissist and the toxic abuser wants to control you. This means he wants to know what is going on with you all the time. You will be questioned incessantly. Regardless of your answer, you will receive doubt to what you said. You will be expected to provide additional explanations. You will find yourself tripping over your tongue because of worry and anxiety hoping he believes you. If he is your spouse, you are supposed to be partnering together in a healthy manner. If you are in a toxic relationship, you will eventually realize you must defer to him as an authoritative role. The reality is that YOU are the boss of your life. You don't need to ask permission or check in with the toxic abuser.

Persistent – The narcissist is extremely persistent during the initial stages of your relationship, during the love bombing. He must have you. It will seem flattering and maybe even endearing. This persistence will stop on a dime. You will end up being confused as he quickly retreats to distance himself while calling you unkind names like needy, suffocating, drama. He created this intensely close relationship dynamic. He pushed your boundaries. Now you are all in and he is retreating and has turned the tables on you blaming you for this dynamic. You will be confused and your self-esteem will have either deteriorated or will be well on its way to ruination. He will circle back after he has given you the silent treatment or has gone missing in action. He will blame you for his absence or punishments. He will then be persistent in winning you back . . . only to do the cycle all over again to you.

Perspective – Only the narcissist's opinion, or analysis, is the perspective that matters . . . according to the narcissistic individual. Your opinion does not matter. He does not want your opinion. Just listen to his. Facts do not matter to the narcissist. The narcissist will deflect, lie, and change meanings to suit his agenda.

Persuasive – The narcissist wants what he wants. If you don't want it, he will do his best to push your boundaries or change your mind to bend to his will. At first, it may seem charming. Later in the relationship, it may be expected or even a demand. Should the narcissist feel you are not changing your mind, he will become irate with you.

Pervert – Maybe you don't see this displayed publicly, or at the office, but the narcissist is into some bizarre things. He is not satisfied, unfulfilled, and is on the constant search for "more." This includes sexual conquests and behaviors. An excessive, and I mean excessive, use of porn is something that you will discover (or he will outright tell you as if boasting that he pulled it over on you). There are many other ways in which the narcissist tries to push sexual boundaries.

Pessimism – The narcissist fuels doom and gloom scenarios. The narcissist is a dream killer. (Unless it is his dream.) The narcissist appears to be supportive at first, giving the illusion he "believes in you," but will find ways to undermine your efforts. The narcissist does not want you to succeed. The narcissist does not want you to have achievements. The narcissist is not proud of you. The narcissist will sabotage you either physically, mentally, emotionally, or financially. You cannot trust a narcissist to be truly supportive of your work. The narcissist will undermine you with overt pessimism or subtle, passive-aggressive pessimism (which you will be accused of "misunderstanding" or "taking it the wrong way").

Pet – Make no mistake about it, the narcissist will try to destroy you and everything you love. That includes your pets. Take special precaution with your pet when you realize you are dealing with a toxic person. My former toxic husband tried to put our beloved westies to sleep. (Thank heavens the vet rescued my westie babies and saved their little lives.)

Petty – The narcissist will harass you over trivial and meaningless points. Just to prove a point, even if he is totally wrong, he will focus on the most insignificant piece of information. Then he will gaslight, bait and bash you, and make you feel stupid. He is doing this to "put you in your place." He is not a nice person. Leave him!

Physical ailments – The stress of being in a relationship with a narcissist will manifest itself in various ways; one of which is in physical health. On the other hand, the narcissist creates his own long list of physical ailments for attention.

Pining – The narcissist wants you to pine over him. The narcissist wants you to work to receive his attention and affection. The narcissist knows how to make you feel obsessed. The narcissist uses tactics and manipulations to break your self-confidence and self-worth. If you must work for the affection of anyone, you need to get out of the relationship immediately. It is toxic to your health.

Placating – The narcissist expects to be pleased and obeyed at all costs . . . even to the extent of loss of family, friends, and your self-worth. Do not do it! It is one thing to be cooperative. It's another to be forced into adherence to what it is he wants. The narcissist tries to trick you by saying you are being selfish or uncooperative.

Side note: he might even be lying about what it is he says he wants just to ruin your plans, and to break your spirit.

Pleasing – You will never truly please the narcissist. The narcissist simply wants to create havoc in your life. The narcissist will complain that you did this wrong, or you misunderstood that. You are never right. The narcissist is never wrong . . . even when he is. The narcissist is an internally unhappy person. The narcissist wants you to be unhappy and self-doubting too.

Poison – The narcissist is toxic—dangerous to your emotional health. The more things you believe about yourself that the narcissist is trying to convince you of, the weaker emotionally you will become. Don't drink the Kool-Aid. Get out of this relationship as soon as you can. Seek help in improving your self-esteem. Even if you think you have a healthy sense of esteem, the narcissist has planted seeds of doubt in your mind.

Police – The abusive individual will bait and bash you, provoke you. If you react, or engage in his abusive crazymaking, suddenly you will hear the abusive person telling you he is calling the police against you. This is why you must leave when any sort of crazymaking, gaslighting, a threat to your freedom, a threat to your safety is made. The abuser will lie to the police and authorities to gain control over you. This tactic, using the courts, attorneys, authorities, managers, and other people is called "abuse by proxy." The courts, attorneys, police can only respond to the information they are given. If they hear only from the abuser, because you are afraid or confused, then you are going to be painted as a villain. You need to leave this toxic person as soon as crazymaking begins. Protect yourself and go no contact. If you are in danger, you should contact the police. If you have been struck, hurt, grabbed, tossed, inappropriately penetrated with a body part, object (knife, etc.), take pictures as you call the police and, if necessary, an ambulance.

Pompous – The narcissist is condescending. The narcissist thinks he is superior over you, and over most others. He may be there helping you in person, but he will make fun of you, your friends, your family in private to gain a feeling of superiority. He will laugh at you and others behind your backs.

Poser (poses as a helper) – He is a fake. Can I be any clearer than that? He is a fake. Most anything he does that appears to be from the goodness or kindness from his heart has strings or an agenda attached to it. He may want accolades. There is something that is fitting into his agenda. He is not sincere.

Positive reinforcement – The narcissist requires a great deal of positive reinforcement and ego stroking.

Positivity – You may be a positive, optimistic individual. The narcissist wants to break that awesome spirit inside of you. You will be ridiculed and belittled for your positivity. Leave any relationship in which you are devalued for any reason whatsoever.

Possessive – The narcissist is jealous of everyone with whom you come in contact. The narcissist is jealous of things you have as well as the belongings of other people. If your success is not undermined or slandered behind your back by the narcissist, then he will claim possession of your success. After all, your success is because of him. He does not love you. Possessive jealousy or jealous possessiveness (either way) is not love. To be clear, the narcissist sees you as an object belonging to him.

Pouts – If the narcissist does not receive the attention he feels he deserves, he will pout. He will behave childishly—like a spoiled toddler. If you neglect to acknowledge this immature behavior, the narcissist will find a way to bait and bash you.

Power – The narcissist wants control over everything. The narcissist thinks this is achieved by having power . . . more and more power. (He's wrong.) The narcissist wants control and power over you as well. He won't be aggressive about it at first. He is clever and slick. Control over you will be strategic. It will happen little by little . . . like a frog in a pot of boiling water.

Praise – The narcissist expects praise for everything. Ev-er-y-th-in-g! If you "neglect" to praise the narcissist for big things, little things, normal things, whatever he wants, he will punish you in some way. (Let's say you didn't praise him for taking out the garbage. Oh noooooo. There will be at least pouting. Perhaps there will be snarky comments. He may even take it to rage and the silent treatment.)

Preachy – Oh Dear God . . . Yes, yes he is. If he is religious, then you have a special blend of a jerk. The Bible states the man is the head and the woman must submit to her husband. (Ask me how I know. Ugh.) The narcissist will use his religious righteousness to dominate you to make you feel inferior.

Predator – The narcissist will prey on your weaknesses and will exploit them.

Preservation – The narcissist is consumed with the need to preserve himself, his beliefs, his actions, his behaviors, at the expense of you and others. You are only a pawn in his life and are easily disposable and replaced.

Pressure – If you do not give into the narcissist's demands, asks, needs, wants, desires, you will be pressured to do so through guilt, shame, gaslighting, manipulation.

Pretentious – This is part of the narcissist's hook: he gives off the illusion and lie of being more important than he truly is. If you discover his lies, the narcissist will turn it around on you saying you are a gold-digger, only like important people, etc.

Prideful – Oh my. A person from the outside looking in might mistake this as "confidence." Prideful is far from being confident. Prideful falls on the side of arrogance.

Priorities – You are not a priority to the narcissist. Your goals and achievements are also competitive priorities to the narcissist's priorities. Therefore, the narcissist will undermine and/or degrade and/or ignore your priorities. The priorities aren't his so they aren't important. The only thing that is a priority for the narcissist is his own agenda.

Prisoner of war – The manipulations, toxic tactics, emotional abuse (as well as other forms of abuse), games, demands, and so on will strip away your self-confidence and self-esteem. You will want out of the abusive relationship, but you won't know how to emotionally break free. You will not know how to leave because you are so dependent on this toxic individual. You will feel like you are a prisoner of the narcissist. You will feel like you are self-doubting, not good enough, worthless person no one would ever love . . . except for him. You may even get to the point in which you do not trust your own decisions for anything because the narcissist has stripped you of your confidence and personality. You might feel like the shell of a person. You are not alone. There is help for narcissistic abuse syndrome and for post-traumatic stress disorder. Seek help in recovering from this abusive relationship. You cannot do this on your own. You need an expert or a specialist.

Problems – The narcissist will create so many problems for you. The narcissist will want YOU to solve all of his problems. The narcissist will BLAME all his problems on you. The narcissist is a problem builder. He will compound a problem with more problems, with more problems, with more problems. There is never a solution in sight. There are only problems and blame and they are all headed in your direction.

Progressive – Suddenly, you wonder what has happened with relationships with family, children, relatives, friends, workmates, and church. Suddenly, you wonder what has happened to your emotions, to your finances, to your life. Subtly the narcissist takes away your self-worth. Subtly the narcissist breaks your boundaries. Subtly the narcissist makes little changes in how you think. It's not really "all of a sudden." This grooming and conditioning has been happening from the very moment the narcissist met you.

Projects and projection – The narcissist always gives himself away through his projections. The narcissist does not see his own faults or shortcomings. The narcissist displaces his own feelings of guilt and unworthiness onto you. The statements the narcissist claims about you might not even make sense; they are simply stated (or shouted) as if true. Generally, these things are true, but not because of your actions; but, because of the narcissist. The narcissist places his own traits onto his victims in an abusive manner. The narcissist continues badgering the victim, using projections, until the victim submits and feels shame.

Promiscuous – Sexual conquests make the narcissist feel significant. The narcissist is always searching for the next best thing. If the narcissist has tricked someone into thinking he is in a committed relationship, the narcissist will cheat. The narcissist does this because the narcissist can, and the narcissist wants to have that feeling of getting one over on you. The narcissist wants to feel superior over you. The narcissist is so arrogant that he can make you believe that 1. He didn't do it and you are creating drama, He can lie to your face and you will simply accept it, 3. You made him do it – it's your fault this happened and you need to do better. The narcissist is developmentally immature and uses sex to feel better about himself. This is not someone you want in your life. Leave the narcissist and don't look back . . . but DO get tested for STDs.

Promises – The narcissist makes empty promises. If you expect the narcissist to follow through with a promise, he will tell you that somehow you were mistaken with the "promise," or there was no promise at all.

Propositions – The narcissist will engage, flirt, and woo others behind your back while he "says" he loves you and that you are the only one. He is lying. The narcissist does not care if the others he engages, flirts, and woos are single, taken, engaged, or married. My former husband was married to me. His married mistress coworker was married too. He did not care. His married girlfriend was a challenge. He got what he wanted. His married girlfriend away from her husband. (He married her shortly after the divorce was granted.) "Soulmates." That game was played. Be careful when someone knows you are in a relationship with someone else and does not respect your boundaries or the boundaries of decency. It says a lot about that person's character that the person would pursue you even when you are wearing an engagement or wedding ring. It is not flattering. It is a game. And you are the pawn. Do not fall for his foolish whispers.

Provocative – This is a deliberate action. The narcissist pokes and provokes on purpose and will say that you misunderstood, or got it wrong. Of course, according to the narcissist, "you" are to blame.

Provokes then blames – This is the same as bait and bash but in nicer words.

Psychological help – The narcissist will ask you for help to "be better" or to "fix" him. This is a manipulation. Don't fall for it. The narcissist cannot and will not change because ultimately, he does not believe there is anything wrong with him. It's all you.

■ The narcissist will twist and blame shift onto you so much you might believe there is something terribly wrong with you. The narcissist will reinforce this. The narcissist will attempt to "fix" you to help you to become "better." He is brainwashing you and systematically putting you under his control. He is not qualified to "fix" anyone.

■ The narcissist will attend sessions to create an illusion of change. The narcissist will take psychological terms used in the sessions against you. The narcissist will say he doesn't need to attend sessions after only two or three sessions claiming he is cured or there was nothing wrong with him at all in the first place. He may even tell you the therapist or psychologist is impressed by him. This is either an out and out lie; or, he believes his delusional tale.

Puppet – The narcissist wants to control you like a puppeteer controls a puppet. You're a fun toy at first, but then if you don't behave exactly as the narcissist wants you to behave, he will put you, his puppet, in a dusty, dirty old box while he plays with new, shiny toys. You deserve better than that. Cut the cords to this twisted puppeteer.

Pursuer – The narcissist is beyond insistent on being with you. He will be overly attentive during the love bombing stage and when he gives breadcrumbs during other stages. He comes after you doggedly. After he has you and begins chipping away at your self-esteem and self-worth, then it all changes. You will begin to feel alone, confused, needy, out of sorts. This is part of the narcissist's strategy in ruining your self-confidence.

Push and blame – Blame on you is used often by the narcissist. With push and blame, the toxic person will push you away emotionally or will create an argument in which you are left feeling abandoned; and then the narcissist will blame you for not being there for him. It is a crazymaking, frustrating manipulation meant to instill loyalty to the narcissist, as well as being there for his every whim. This is exhausting for the target.

PTSD – Post Traumatic Stress Disorder – Narcissistic abuse is likely to leave you with PTSD. You must seek help to fully heal. PTSD is not something you can manage to heal on your own.

Public image – The narcissist doesn't mind hurting you, being abhorrent in private. In public, or with people he wants to fool and/or impress, he is a different person than the one you see. The narcissist can maintain a false image for long periods of time. He's a charmer, and "a saint" to everyone else who can save the day. He likes being called upon to handle things and will do tasks in a seemingly helpful and cooperative manner. Later, the narcissist will complain-boast at length like a martyr at how he is the only one to tackle the issues.

Punishment – The narcissist, as well as all toxic people, love to inflict various types of punishments on the targets. Punishments are not appropriate in adult relationships. In adult relationships, rational and calm communication is appropriate. The punishment the narcissist doles out on you does not match the "slight" of which you are being accused. Under no circumstances, when you are in a mature relationship with someone, are punishments ever appropriate. If you find yourself being punished, then you need to leave this unbalanced relationship. You need to seek help to regain your self-esteem.

Punitive – The narcissist will impose punishments he deems will put you in your place.

Puppet – A narcissist will expect you to do what he wants, behave as he wants, and perform as he wants. You are his puppet. The narcissist wants you to support his career (to the point where you must find employment for him), support him in all aspects. Note, he will not do the same for you. He is slick in his convincing, holier than thou, more intelligent than you attitude. He will make you believe if you don't like what he likes, or watch him do his tasks (including every sport he likes, every activity or whim he has) then he will leave you in the dust. And he will. The narcissist is that arrogant.

Pushy – The narcissist is rather aggressive and forceful in challenging your beliefs, your way of life, in and making you dependent on him. The narcissist is also pushy toward others in the service industry, or with employees and coworkers he deems "beneath" him.

Q

Question – If you question the narcissist, the narcissist sees this as an attack (even if the question is a generic one). The narcissist will reply with a snide attitude, or snarky (at the lower end of meanness) to all-out aggression, anger, and even abuse (at the higher end of the trigger). To the narcissist, if you question him, that means you are attacking him. Because he has escalated your question as a direct "attack" on him, you instantly become the enemy and will be treated as such. The narcissist does not like any type of question. (The narcissist is firm in his paranoid belief into thinking you have an evil agenda.) You will soon learn you are not allowed to ask questions. Should you remain, you will become an excessive worrier and self-questioner.

Questioning – The narcissist will question you, your whereabouts, your intentions, your actions, your privacy, your schedule, your methods, and so on endlessly. The questions usually turn in to disgust by the narcissist. The narcissist may even elevate the disgust to anger and rage.

Questions – Did you have plans with the narcissist? Were you excited about an event that you talked about all week? When the event is upon you, the narcissist may ask, "Are we still doing that?" You may think, "Seriously?" but you know you dare not say that word. Instead, you are put on the defensive having to provide reasons why you want to attend the event. He is doing this because he does not want to go to the activity. He wants to do something else. He may even be so gracious as to give his blessing to you to go with your friends. Ohhhhh, be careful! That, too, is a trick. You going with your friends will be used against you in the future. He may "question" what you are making for dinner because he does not want it. He may "question" your outfit or hair because he wants to hurt your feelings. The sneaky snake snarky questions have a purpose and that purpose is to make you feel bad. Flee from this jerk and seek help from a professional.

Quickly turn and run as soon as you realize you are in a relationship with a narcissist.

R

Rabbit hole – Crazymaking. The narcissist wants you to question yourself about most everything. Instilling self-doubt in your abilities is the narcissist's secret weapon.

Rages – The narcissist will go levels beyond angry into a rage like you've never seen. It's scary. If you are a panic laugher like I am, you better duck or run for cover. The narcissist might become physically abusive. The narcissistic rage is terrifying . . . and is meant to terrorize you. Get a protection from abuse order. Go no contact. Never speak or communicate with this person ever again for any reason whatsoever.

Rationalize – The narcissist will righteously justify his actions as being superior, forth-right, even noble (even if the actions were rage-driven, out of control, or rude). While the narcissist is righteously justifying his actions away (for example, "you made him do it"), he neglectfully accepts any responsibility. He will sidestep taking ownership by twisting facts.

Raw – Frazzled. Emotional. Vulnerable. Torn apart emotionally. Do you feel like this? Do you feel raw, lost, alone, and like a shell because of all the worry and self-doubt? The narcissist is working his crazymaking on you. He is chipping away at your insecurities to damage your self-confidence and self-worth. The only way to make this feeling end and to regain your authentic self is to remove yourself from the situation, seek help from a specialist, and go no contact from this abuser. Never speak to him again.

Reaction – The narcissist wants to provoke a reaction from you. Don't give him one. The narcissist will try to engage you in his crazymaking. The narcissist will blindside you with bizarre accusations that he wants you to explain, and even defend. He will bait and bash you, provoke you, and then blame you for reacting to his abuse. If you find yourself engaged, just stop. Stop right then and there. Don't follow the crazy train the narcissist is conducting.

Read between the lines – The narcissist is evasive; therefore, you are constantly expected to read between the lines of his communication. Ultimately you will infer the wrong meaning, which in turn will cause problems.

Reasoning – Forget about it. You cannot reason with a narcissist. The narcissist can and will use everything you say against you.

Reassurance – Forget about getting reassurance from a narcissist, or toxic individual. The narcissist will not give you reassurances when you need it most. It will make you feel out of control. It will make you feel so sad and low, even worthless when the narcissist in your life withholds affection and reassurances of love and kindnesses. The narcissist knows this and will purposefully withhold it from you. The narcissist does not love you, care about you, or what you are going through so trying to appeal to an emotional side is pointless. The narcissist will appear annoyed at your many attempts to have a sliver of reassurance but enjoys watching you fall apart. Get out of this toxic relationship. Seek help in rebuilding your self-worth and self-esteem.

Recovery – You have been abused emotionally and mentally if you have been in a relationship with a narcissist which is very damaging to your own sense of self. The abuse may have also resulted in sexual, financial, and so on. The very first step in your recovery is to go no contact. That means, do not, for any reason at all—AT ALL—contact the narcissist. Do not reply to the narcissist. Do not find a reason to contact the narcissist to "remind" him about something "important." No contact means no contact. It is the only way to begin healing and lead to recovery. To recover from narcissistic abuse, and likely PTSD, it is encouraged you seek help from a professional specializing in narcissistic abuse. You may want to participate in a group focusing on recovery from narcissistic abuse.

Red flags – Your inner voice will tell you something is not right. You hear your inner voice telling you these things. LISTEN to your inner voice. Your inner voice will throw red flag warnings to you intuitively. Your inner voice will let you know when something is not right with the situation, but with this person. I am stressing to you that you need to LISTEN to the inner voice! Do not make excuses. Do not justify his negative attitude. When he shows you who he is, you need to believe it!

Red Riding Hood – Red Riding Hood fell victim to a monster who posed to be kind, and attentive. Fortunately, someone figured out he was a wolf in grammie's clothing. This is the story of the narcissist. In the original version, the narcissist wolf "eats her up." (Sound familiar? Do you feel as if you are being devoured?) In a modern version, the woodsman saves her and the grandmother. I would say it took a village to help Red Riding Hood recover.

Reflection – The narcissist wants to see you being who he wants you to be. You must be what he wants at ALL TIMES. The narcissist wants you to reflect the image that he has created; that he is in control of. The reflection he wants to see is of himself. You reflect him. Should you displease him, a narcissistic event, or manipulation, or belittling, perhaps rage, will occur.

Reinforcement – The narcissist is not nice. The narcissist gets a fix, or reinforcement for his behavior, in watching you fall, in his rages, in his outbursts, in manipulating you to engage with his crazymaking. All the awful things you are experiencing have been orchestrated by the narcissist in your life . . . and he is relishing it. The narcissist is also getting reinforcement from his flying monkeys. This may hurt you or make you feel sad. Get help for recovery because really whatever these types of people have to say is worthless and nonsense. The proof is in the pudding of who you are, who the narcissist is, and who the flying monkey mouthpieces are.

Rejection – Because of abandonment issues, rejection is a weakness most likely for you. People who are weak emotionally, for whatever reason, are prone to sadnesses and not feeling as though they measure up. You might tell the narcissist how a loved one left and it hurt (such as a parent leaving when and you were devastated, or a friend died suddenly without you being prepared for it, or perhaps a family members death, maybe during a difficult time people had to choose sides and you lost loved ones). The narcissist will use rejection feeling and abandonment against you. It is a favorite tactic of the narcissist. It is a manipulation to instill fear and to prove loyalty to the narcissist so he would "never" leave me and to make me feel inferior to him. An over-abundance of people pleasing is used.

■ Rejection 2 – Should you finally arrive at the point where you are no longer going to take the narcissist's abuse and "reject" the bull the narcissist is serving, watch out! The narcissist will amp up his efforts to hurt you, to bait and bash you, to provoke you, will unleash his flying monkeys on you, and will greatly over-react (while blaming you for the overreaction). Some people will walk out of your life because of things the narcissists have said and "proved" about you. Let them go. Do not try to stop them. If they can't see through the narcissist's crazymaking, let them walk. You may choose to walk away from some people who were in your life. Do it. Your emotional wellbeing is so much more important than trying to people please. (People pleasing is not pleasing at all.) Go not contact the crazy maker. Change all your passwords. Cancel your credit cards and order new ones. Seek help in recovering from emotional abuse.

Relationships – The narcissist cheats in all relationships. The narcissist does not really want to be in a relationship. The narcissist wants to dominate and control. You are not in a relationship of mutual love, respect, admiration. Just get out of this toxic farce and go no contact.

■ One of the few types of people who enjoy being friends with a narcissist, surprisingly, is another narcissist. They are both self-righteous. Let them implode in their own self-righteous and superiority over all others. They are not even loyal to their other narcissist friends. It is a bizarre cycle of friendship. They talk about each other, undercut each other, sabotage each other, set each other up, and make fun of each other behind each other's backs.

■ Another type of person who will try to be a friend or in a relationship with a narcissist is someone who has low self-esteem and easily puts people on a pedestal and has admiration of others issue.

Relentless – Oh the narcissist never stops. Just when you think you are at a good place, bam. Out of left field comes the topic and problem you thought was over . . . long over . . . solved. Not to the toxic narcissist. If the narcissist is not getting his own way, the topic will be addressed over and over and over again until you cave in, give up, and submit.

Relocating blame – The narcissist will shift blame onto you; will project his issues onto you. The narcissist takes no ownership of wrongdoings. According to the narcissist, it's your fault. The narcissist will find the most minute reason for this to be so, or will make it up, will lie, will change or skew the facts altogether. The narcissist avoids all self-reflection of issues, misbehavior, unkindnesses, abuses, and loss of control. When you realize what the narcissist is doing, you need to leave the relationship. It will not get better.

Reminisces – The narcissist lives in the past. He will speak of the glory days often. This happens because he is emotionally and developmentally stuck in the past. This is a clue, a pathetic one, so take note. If you hear an overindulging amount of glory days' chatter, you need to realize he is emotionally stuck. You will probably see the narcissist's childish temper tantrums next. Run! Get out! He is an immature, mean-spirited, wants-his-own way man-child.

Remorse – The narcissist does not feel regret or remorse. He is unable to feel emotion toward another person's feelings. He may fake it, but he cannot feel it and quite frankly he does not care. He has no remorse.

Repetition – This goes along with relentless. Until the narcissist gets what he wants, he will continue to bring up the topic he wants you to do (or not do). He wants to not only change your mind but bend your will, break your spirit and put you in your place for defying what he wants.

Replies – The narcissist is on his very own time schedule. He will not reply to you when he reads your text, email, or hears a voicemail when he sees/hears it. You are insignificant to him and he wants you to know this subconsciously. You will have to wait an inordinate amount of time for the reply. You may want to text again, or call, or email, but really, if you were important to him, you would receive a reply . . . something. It takes seconds to reply and the narcissist knows it and just does not care. If the narcissist does reply, and you need an answer or direction to something, he will make sure to be evasive, or avoid an answer. You will notice that you may even receive both way answers in a confusing conversation. That way whatever it is you do, you will be wrong.

Repress – You are expected to push down sad feelings and not talk about how you feel to the narcissist, or to anyone. The narcissist does not want you to be you. The narcissist wants you to be what he wants you to be. You are not supposed to air issues outside of him. The narcissist wants you to keep the abuse to yourself. He does not care about how you are feeling; therefore, he certainly doesn't want you to bring it up. (After all, he said he was sorry (in an insincere, unapologetic way, in no way taking responsibility).)

Rescue – He will set up situations in which he needs to be rescued and only you can rescue them. The narcissist will create an illusion that will make you feel needed. You will feel as if only you can help him. This is a trick to make you codependent in the relationship. He may even tell you that if you cannot help him, he will find someone else. (But wait, you are the only one who could help him. Right? Wrong. He has a stable of others he can call upon if you fail to please him. It was a test. All the tasks are tests to prove your loyalty to him.)

Rescuer – The narcissist sets his sights on someone who is vulnerable. This may mean significant years younger, disabled, newly broken up, etc. The narcissist feels better if he can rescue this person. After the illusion of rescuing his victim, he will begin to torment the one he rescued. The narcissist is not a prize, a prince, or Prince Charming. He's a der.

■ After the narcissist has dumped you, punished you, or has withdrawn affection from you several times, and you begin to catch on, the narcissist will admit there is something wrong with him and he needs help. He appears to reach out to you giving you the opportunity to rescue. This is a trick. Do not fall for it. The narcissist does need help. He will never actually get help because the narcissist doesn't truly believe there is anything wrong with him.

Resentful – If you are getting attention for a job well done, receiving praise for an accomplishment, or working on a goal of yours, the narcissist will become resentful about it and will demean, and make whatever it is you've done (your positive or your win) into something ugly, negative and will accuse you of seeking attention and being showy.

Resilient – The narcissist overcomes things because there does not seem to be an internal measure of reflection he uses to gauge himself. After he dumps you, he has another chick already waiting. After he bankrupts you, he pulls up his money reserve goes on vacation and buys a new house. After he has you removed from the job, he goes for a promotion. The narcissist just bounces on to the next thing. Bounce, bounce, bounce. It is what he does. He creates a mess and bounces on to the next thing.

Respect – The narcissist expects your obedience as respect. If you fail to be obedient, the narcissist will accuse you of being disrespectful. If you do anything the narcissist doesn't like or finds fault with, the narcissist will say you are disrespectful. If you do not support every whim and every part of the narcissist, he will harass you saying you are disrespectful. The narcissist's motto and creed are that it's all about him (the narcissist). The narcissist does not respect you and will not give you respect. The narcissist will not show you respect. Don't expect respect after he has you captured in his web. You must break free from this toxic relationship.

Revenge – Revenge is for the weak. Guess who is weak and pathetic. The narcissist is. During your relationship, he probably boasted of tales of how he had revenge (most likely in a passive aggressive way like a coward) from those he thought "wronged" him. Guess who else he will use revenge on. You! The narcissist will use revenge to punish you and to control you. This is one of the reasons you need to go no contact, do not engage with the narcissist at all, and seek help to navigate your way through the narcissistic minefield after care.

Righteous justification – The narcissist not only justifies his negative behavior and actions, he takes it to an entirely new level of being morally right, even virtuous. Meanwhile, the narcissist, while being morally correct, is slaughtering your healthy opinions and behaviors by throwing in bizarre and twisted opinions that do not make any sense. For example: if you believe women should be CEO's, then you believe all men should have breasts. Wait, what? The narcissist will then take off on some outlandish rationale scenario he makes up as what it is you believe and will assign that belief to you as having said this, or that it is your true belief that he figured out.

Righteousness – Oh dear God. The narcissist is above all others in his morality . . . or so he believes. He will use his righteous morality to belittle you and put you down. He will use his righteous morality to put down family, friends, coworkers. Any reason to pull out the righteous morality card, he will use it. After all, he knows best. (Ha! What a jerk!)

Rigid – The narcissist is rigid with his own self-serving rules and rituals. If you annoy him or he wrongly believes you are attempting to impose on his time or his ritual (like he does while the boundary breaks through your comfort levels) he will rage against you. (This is also an example of blame shifting.) A narcissist requires constant attention (when he's with you) or else he will become resentful and mean-spirited.

Ringtone – Each of the narcissist's side chicks in his book has a special ringtone, and not necessarily a name attached to the number. You can google the seemingly endless miscellaneous numbers that just happen to call the narcissist's phone. Or, why bother. Once you figure it out, just leave. You're not special. You are not "the only girl in the world" to the narcissist. You are just one of many. Remember, he does not love you and never will. He does not love you. He does not love you. You are not his soulmate. The narcissist has songs for all his side pieces so they feel special too. It's an illusion. (Just like his feelings towards you.) The narcissist wants you to bring up the endless unidentified numbers so the narcissist can argue with you and gaslight you into believing you are paranoid, crazy, causing drama. Just leave the "relationship" and go no contact. (He does not love you!)

Risky – The narcissist may want you to engage in risky behavior (to prove your loyalty, to have something on you in which to manipulate you, and/or control you). You need to hold true to your boundaries. If you hold true to your boundaries, no one can make you do anything you don't want to do. If you are the target of the narcissist, then your boundaries will be tested. If you are feeling shame, or guilt after doing something for your narcissistic partner you would have never done previously because you have broken your boundaries for him, and now you are afraid because he is blackmailing you. YOU put it out there first. You become the controller of the information. YOU handle it. Seek help to do this in a safe, healthy, ethical, and legal way; but take back your control and power nonetheless.

Roots – The narcissist's behavior is not caused by you or anything you did or did not do for or to the narcissist. The narcissist's behavior goes back to his childhood and is rooted in that period. There is nothing you, as a layperson, can do to change or fix the narcissist. You simply need to leave the toxic relationship and seek help in healing from the narcissistic abuse.

Rude – When the narcissist is love bombing you, he is a charmer. You will overlook, or may not see, rude and boorish behaviors at first. They are there and they will surface. There is a misguided sense of entitlement that is harsh. The behavior is rude. The rude behaviors will be directed at staff, others, you, and people you care about, either right to their faces or behind their backs. The rude behavior will most likely be blamed on you. You will be left with that "what just happened" feeling; or the "wait, how is this my fault?' feeling. That's a red flag you need to notice.

Rules – The narcissist will impose rules on you. Your strict adherence to the rules is expected by the narcissist. These rules can and will change often to throw you off balance, demean you, confuse you, and to put you under the control of the narcissist.

Ruthless – The narcissist lacks empathy, caring, and compassion. The narcissist is ruthless in his quest to cause you emotional pain to control you. He is always scheming and strategizing how he will chip away at your self-worth.

S

Sabotage – What do you love? Be prepared to have it ruined. The narcissist will plant seeds of doubt in you, your self-worth, and your accomplishments (anything of which you are proud). Want to kick a bad habit? The narcissist will make it easy for you to have/do what you want to eliminate from your life. Want to improve? Not while the narcissist will distract you, belittle you, make you prove loyalty to him over your self-improvement work. What holidays do you like celebrating? Don't bother buying anything for him. Do you think he bought anything for you? If you think that, you are fooling yourself. He is not going to give you something that would make you happy. The narcissist will most likely break up with you (or be mad at you) around all holidays. The bigger of importance the holiday is, the more you need to expect to be alone (even if he is physically there beside you). Thanksgiving, Christmas, Valentine's Day seem to be disappointing for me and the narcissist. I made excuses why there was no gift, why we weren't celebrating. I didn't say I was being punished for "my" bad behavior (turning the tables on me and blaming me). Birthdays: well, my family loved celebrating birthdays so even if he was mad at me for whatever reason, I still had presents and cake . . . and denial. (Yell at me on my birthday? What a jerk.)

Sadistic – The narcissist is sadistic. The narcissist gains a superior feeling, a pleasurable feeling, from destroying another person emotionally, mentally, and financially. This pleasure is done through systematic and strategic tactics used by the personality disordered narcissist.

Safety – You need to document everything the narcissist does and share it with professionals (like the police and counselors). Create a safety plan with friends and family. The plan is for your physical safety and emotional wellness. (The withdrawal after a toxic relationship can be like drug withdrawal.) Secure your home. Change the locks, buy bolts, buy interior and exterior video cameras, and purchase exterior movement lights. Change your coming and going patterns. Stay away from places you went together. Stay off social media for a while after you block him, his flying monkeys, his friends, and family. Change all your passwords, email if necessary. Call the banks and inform them of the possibility of what this person could possibly do to harm your credit. Change your credit cards. Remove him from all finances and investments. Change your banking. Change your phone number if necessary. Take his name off of your emergency contacts. Have a male escort to and from your car at work, fitness center, and the grocery store (any place you frequent).

Saint – People will think he's a saint. Like the chameleon, he takes on the colors (traits) of those around him to blend in . . . fit in. This helps him to pull off his "nice guy" act to manipulate you and those around you. The thing is, you helped create the illusion for others to believe by keeping quiet about the abuse happening to you. Speak up! When others hear how he really is, some won't believe you (let them walk), some will say they knew something was "off" about him, and some will totally understand. Share your story. He isn't a saint, and he isn't as gentle as a dove. He is a fake. He is a liar. He does not love you. He never has. He has no loyalty to you. Stop protecting him because he is most definitely not protecting your dignity. He wants to destroy you and your self-worth.

Sanity – When you are in a relationship with a narcissist, you will feel as though you have lost your mind.

Sarcastic – The narcissist uses sarcasm to mock, belittle, cut you down to size, and put you in your place. It's not a nice thing to do at all. To me, it shows the abuser has no real basis to argue with you so he must use the childish, low level, immature behavior of sarcasm. The narcissist, after all, is emotionally immature; therefore, he will argue like an angry child or a teen or throw temper tantrums like a toddler.

Savage – The emotional abuse (and perhaps physical abuse) is methodical, strategic, and savage. You will feel torn apart, ripped apart—like a tiger does to his prey.

Save him – He wants you to help him. He wants you to save him because you are the only one who understands him. He will use your helping, empathic, compassionate nature (combined with your vulnerability and low self-esteem) to save him from himself and miraculously turn him into a "worthy" person. (Oh please! This is a con! This is an act! You and your emotions are a game to him.)

Savior – Depending on the type of narcissist you are dealing with, you will be sucked into the narcissist's life by either "being saved" or by "being the savior." No one can save you but you. Conversely, you cannot save anyone else. It's up to the other individual to change his life. If you are in a "being saved" or "being the savior" dynamic, you are in an unbalanced relationship which will not end well for you. Get out now and find your emotional equal. The narcissist is not it. The narcissist's emotional maturity is stunted in his youth. It could be childhood or teen years. The narcissist does not have a normal adult's emotional maturity. (Wonder why older people are with people noticeably younger than themselves? It is emotional immaturity. The "young one" is with the emotionally immature person for her own twisted issues.) If the narcissist throws your age in your face, let this be a red flag to you of the narcissist's immature emotional development. Laugh to yourself at him as you walk out the door.

■ The narcissist is not your savior for any issue. The narcissist will use your issue, your weaknesses, to hurt you and destroy you. Seek help in healing these issues to become empowered.

Scared – The narcissist's agenda, and whatever is on it, is special or sacred to him. That could include still needing to please his parents, his relatives, his religion, his boss, and show them his self-worth. He is using you to give credibility to his twisted false self-esteem personality.

Scheme – The narcissist is a schemer. The narcissist always has some sort of scheme up his sleeve. It is a scheme that will make you feel bad, that's for sure.

Secure – A secure person does not seduce another man's wife and/or coworker. A secure person doesn't abuse the pets, children, members of the family. A secure person doesn't need flying monkeys or a harem. A secure person doesn't have porn, drug, alcohol, sex, alternate world video addictions. A secure person does not empty the bank account from his unemployed wife, nor does he hide assets. A secure person does not use the workplace as his dating hookup site. A secure person does not blame other people. A secure person takes ownership for his role in the issue. A secure person asks for forgiveness and knows how to sincerely and genuinely apologize. A secure person trusts. A secure person doesn't need admiration from everyone.

Seducer – You are a challenge for the narcissist. He wants to possess you and to control you for no other reason than to feed his ego. He does not follow the rules of decency or society. He makes up his own "justifications" for his behavior (most of which make him the "righteous victim" in his tales of woe). Eventually, he will take your money, cheat on you, destroy you emotionally, and move on to the next target. It's what he does. Do not let him back into your life! Go no contact. Seek help for recovery from specialists.

Self-absorbed – More than you can imagine.

Self-care – You must go no contact to heal. You need help to work through narcissistic abuse. You need help to become empowered. You need to learn coping skills to avoid narcissistic abuse triggers. You may even need help to overcome PTSD. Narcissistic abuse is serious. A relationship with a narcissist is unlike any other relationship you've ever had.

Self-centered – The world revolves around him. The narcissist puts himself first above all others.

Self-confidence – The narcissist will destroy, shatter, and ruin your self-confidence. The narcissist does this to make himself feel better, feel superior over his victims . . . over you. To the narcissist, you are no different from any object that can be tossed aside easily.

Self-hate – The narcissist wants you to feel as bad as he does. The narcissist wants you to hate yourself. The narcissist will use manipulations, comparisons, blame, accusations, and so on to make you self-question yourself and plant seeds of doubt about your very existence. If you feel as though you hate yourself, this person is not the answer for you. This is a toxic person. You need to leave this relationship and seek help in rebuilding your esteem and learn to love yourself again.

Self-image – The narcissist has a poor self-image which is why he fabricates one. He creates a mythical world where he is important and often saves the day. The narcissist wants to destroy your self-image using your weaknesses. This is done using manipulations to make you feel inferior so he can feel superior over you.

Self-important – The narcissist may or may not have a truly important position. It does not matter really because he is the most important person he knows.

Self-love – The narcissist does not love himself and he does not love you. I tried practicing loving myself enough to ask for what I wanted. Oh boy, did the narcissist turn the tables on that. He called me demanding. I had earned an impressive achievement. I was excited. I told him about it. Instead of being happy for me, I was interrogated. There was no celebration or surprise present to mark the event. I mustered up my bravery and asked him if we were going to celebrate. He was silent. Seething. Then it turned into me making demands and nothing he did was ever good enough for me. (Um, there was nothing at all and this was a pretty big deal.) Eventually, it turned into his "latest illness" and how I do not care about him. Days later I asked if I could buy something I wanted. As usual, he was not truly listening to me speak. I went by myself to my favorite local shop and bought a designer necklace. I love it. It marked a success . . . my personal success. He cannot take that away from me – ever.

Self-promoter – The narcissist is always "on." Overtly: he is always working the room. He is always looking for his next challenge or conquest. He uses self-promotion to further his agenda. Covertly: he is working the room in another way. It is subtle. He is watching everyone, listening, "taking it all in" so he can use what he finds out about you and other people. The covert narcissist may seem shy and quiet. Oh no. He has his tactics and they are just as ruthless as the overt narcissist.

Self-rationalization – The narcissist righteously justifies his actions by rationalizing away his misdeed and places blame on you or someone else in his circle. If all else fails, he will tell you that you are responsible for his misdeeds. "YOU made me behave that way." (Seriously?)

Selfish – The narcissist is overly concerned with all things him. He is overly concerned with how everything affects him . . . how everything relates to him. He is fixated on how things play into the narcissist's wants, needs, interests. Your wants and needs do not matter . . . at all. You are not a priority. The narcissist is always running an internal game of self-profiting strategy and moves.

Semantics – Narcissists are clever. He may not strike you, but he will abuse you emotionally and mentally. He will use backhanded compliments to tear you apart. He will degrade you publicly in a joking, funny manner, encouraging you to participate in your own ridicule. There are outright mean statements creatively disguised with nice words. You will wonder "what just happened? Was that mean or nice?" And, of course, there is the way the narcissist can turn the tables on you using his language skills. It's frustrating to the target. It produces worry and anxiety.

Sententious – Pompous, self-righteous, self-important, arrogant, know-it-all, preachy narcissist. (Can I be clearer?) This trait is one that many narcissists have. The narcissist who hides behind religion is especially apt to be sententious over you. (The guy is a blow-hard bore. You can do better with someone who authentically embraces faith. The healthy fella will be a partner with you, not a dominant righteous religious dog.)

Separation anxiety – The narcissist has created this in you. It is pathological. It is not your fault for falling for it. Now that you know, you can avoid this with anyone because you will know what is happening and will realize, "this person is a narcissist. I'm out."

Sex – Apparently sex, meaningless sex with whomever, makes a narcissist feel significant. It doesn't matter if the narcissist is in a "relationship" with you, or someone else, because he will cheat. He cheats to feel important. Sex is a cliché narcissist fix in feeling superior. This is so risky to your health; therefore, if he cheats even one time on you, leave this relationship fast! His cheating is like roaches: when one exposed in the light of day; there are a thousand more hidden behind the walls.

Sex acts – You will think the narcissist is exciting. The narcissist is teaching you to "explore" your sexuality. The abuser will systematically progress into degrading sex acts meant to make you subservient, submissive, degrading, and inferior. Do not be fooled into thinking this is a playful role-playing fantasy. This is the narcissist's real life. (And it is quite likely you are not the only one he is playing these sex games with.) Get out and get checked!

Sexual conquests – Sex gives the narcissist a false sense of being sought after and self-importance. The narcissist pumps up his false ego. Having a stable of sexual conquests available increases his false ego as well. The narcissist does not have an emotional connection to any of the partners. He looks at all of them as pathetic for putting up with his antics. He does not have respect for his conquests. He is not in love with any of them, or you, regardless of what he tells you. Get out now before you contract a disease. Seek help in rebuilding your self-worth.

Sexual disorder – In 1898, according to the physician Havelock Ellis who studied human sexuality, the narcissist-like individual was associated with excessive masturbation because the person becomes his own pleasurable sexual desire. (In my experience and research, the excessive masturbation piece, came up frequently. I was truly surprised especially since a narcissist announced he did it all the time, had a secret life of porn, and was addicted to porn.) This "excessive" disorder follows suit with the story of Narcissus who kept trying to touch and kiss himself and was only enamored by himself.

Shame – Believing that you are unworthy and flawed is implanted onto victims using the victim's own weaknesses. Shame is about "you." (Don't believe it though, the narcissist is using shame as a tactic to discredit "you" directly.) This happens because the victim perceives that she does not have as much power as the abuser. (This also occurs in parent/child, employer/employee, teacher/student, coach/player, and so on relationships.) The victim turns the painful emotions of feeling unworthy, not good enough, flawed inward which turns to guilt, self-blame, self-questioning. Shame is meant to silence you. If someone is shaming you, leave that toxicity.

Shapeshifter – Narcissists are fake. The narcissist does not have an authentic personality of his own. He is like a chameleon who can change from one emotion to another in the blink of an eye.

Sharing feelings – Do not get set up by oversharing because you think he is interested in you. During the first stages of the relationship, the narcissist wants to know all there is about you. He wants to know your feelings. More specifically, he wants to know how your emotions operate. He wants to know how strong/weak you are, and how to trigger various responses from you. After the love stage has eroded, should you try to share your feelings, you will end up in a worse place than when you started. The narcissist diverts the attention onto him and his needs, or onto another subject altogether, all the while offering no reassurance. It is the exact opposite. He wants you to feel guilty. He wants you to feel ashamed. He wants you to feel inferior. He wants you to feel needy. In a normal, balanced, healthy relationship, you are free to share feelings. You need to love yourself enough to ask for whatever emotional needs you want to talk about without fear of being belittled. Having a healthy sense of self-love is not narcissistic; the narcissist will try to demean you by saying YOU are the narcissist is you exert your self-worth and self-confidence. Be proud of yourself and don't let anyone tear you down or make you feel bad for wanting to talk about what you need in a relationship.

Silenced – The narcissist does not want to hear anything you must say because the narcissist does not care about you or your feelings. The narcissist will silence you. You are unimportant after all. END THE SILENCE on ABUSE and DOMESTIC VIOLENCE! Share your story!

Silencing you – The narcissist uses shame, control to silence you. The toxic individual does not want you talking about what is going on with you, or in your mind, with others. The toxic person wants to control and dominate you and your actions. END YOUR SILENCE by SHARING YOUR STORY!

Silent treatment – This is a mean tactic used to put you in your place, manipulate you, control you, prove your loyalty, and undermine you. It is meant to hurt you, make you feel needy, obsessed, and gaslight you. The silent treatment is a favorite tactic of the toxic narcissist and uses it often. Run, don't walk, from anyone who uses the immature, unhealthy, silent treatment on you.

Slanders – Narcissists will backstab you with lies to everyone. The narcissist will tear your character to shreds. The narcissist will assassinate your character. Of course, you know who the narcissist really is behind his normal-person mask. You cannot win against a narcissist. The narcissist is strategic. The narcissist has his flying monkeys do the dirty work for him. The narcissist is skilled at the divide and conquer approach. If you put out one fire the narcissist has created; just wait, there will be another one. My best advice is to walk away. Walk away from the narcissist, walk away from the flying monkeys, walk away from anyone who is not supportive, walk away from anyone who is looking for a scoop to create drama, walk away from anyone who simply does not believe you. They are not worth your time. Wish them well if you want, but walk away and do not look back. Your life will improve and will be filled with better people who want the best for you. It is as if you are dead-heading a flower bed. Get rid of those who look to hurt you for whatever reason, and let the beautiful ones surface, bloom, and flourish.

Small – The narcissist wants you to lose yourself in his world. He wants you focused on his needs, his wants, his desires. Your needs, wants and desires become secondary (ha, who am I kidding. They aren't even secondary. They are last . . . lower than last.) You will begin to feel small, invisible, or insignificant. Your significance will be tied to making sure he is happy and his needs are met. Other than that, you will feel so small and alone . . . because you are. Get out of this relationship. Go no contact. Seek help from a specialist in rebuilding your self-worth.

Smears and smear campaigns – The narcissist will smear you in one way or another. You may not even know what is being said about your behind your back. The narcissist will create lies about you as you are the abuser. The narcissist makes you prove who you are—that you are not abusive or the abusive one in the relationship. The narcissist will make up lies about you and proceed to share those lies himself. Or, the narcissist will "confide" lies about you to others so these people do the dirty work for him. (They would be the narcissist flying monkeys.) Do not fall into the trap of defending yourself. You won't win. Those who believe him, don't belong in your life anyway. You will never have contact with them again. And, if you think you will, again, who cares what they think. You are on your way to healing. Let the haters hate. You know the truth. Do not react to this immature tactic unless it is actionable. If you are damaged financially by the lies, you should consult an attorney.

Social media – The narcissist has more than an average number of selfies for a man on social media. The pictures are usually just of him. He cannot post about other women for fear the others figure out they are being cheated on. He also wants to appear to be available for new prey.

■ The narcissist will demand passwords for all your social media. He will belittle and badger you until you relent. Do not do it! Do give away your passwords, your finances, or your power.

Social media safety – You must change every password for your social media accounts. It would be wise to change your email password; and, call your bank and have new credit cards issued.

■ The narcissist will monitor where you are and with whom on your social media page. If you have the narcissist blocked, he will use his flying monkeys to do his dirty work for him. (The pathetic part is that they do! It is very immature; but, that's on them.)

■ Block and delete the narcissist's friends and family. They are not your friends. They are not your family. The narcissist to find out information on you.

■ Hide your friend list and contact list on all social media. He or his flying monkeys will message your friends in an attempt to smear you.

■ If you do not have the narcissist and his flying monkeys blocked, they will screenshot your social media page, your work history, your status, your relationships, your male friends.

■ BE cautious of new friend requests. Triple check them. It could be a fake account created by the narcissist or one of his flying monkeys. He could pretend he is a female. He could pretend he is a new male friend. You must be very cautious.

■ You must block these people because they can see your friends and family information as well and might be able to pick up clues as to where you are or what you are doing and follow that to figure out all that they can about you.

■ Ask your friends and family to block them as well. If they are supportive, and not part of the flying monkey problem, they will do this in a heartbeat for you and your safety.

Socializing – It is a strain for narcissists to be with groups of people for too long. He doesn't want to be found out. It may be difficult for him to contain himself so he will take off/get out/leave without a logical reason except to put you down in the process of his exit in some way. If you arrived together, the narcissist will throw the departure squarely on your shoulders in front of others, including the host, by projecting what he wants onto you: Are you ready to go? You look bored. You don't seem happy. (You could have been just laughing with someone and the narcissist says this about you. It is projection.) Then there is the inability for him to behave appropriately in certain situations. Perhaps the narcissist is bored at the funeral reception. (Notice if he starts talking about himself or his work, or his sports. He is bored because the attention is off of him.) Maybe people are connecting with you at your reunion, he will find a way to take the attention, an inappropriate way that will embarrass you. There is shaming by the narcissist too. If he is not the center of attention, the narcissist will shame you for staying too long, talking too much, and attach it to some suspicious hidden agenda reason in which to blame you. If it is his event that he wants to attend or his family activities, the same things may happen. He will purposefully leave you so you feel uncomfortable and alone. It's funny for him. It's a game. It's pathetic and rude. You do not need that.

■ If you are at an event together, expect to be ignored. Perhaps you are at his work event. You will likely see him flirting with others. You may not know anyone. That doesn't matter to him. He will walk off and leave you on your own. If you are at his family event, he will leave you alone when you know no one (and you've asked in advance for him to stay with you).

■ Yes, you arrived together at a social event, perhaps a work Christmas party where he is drinking. He will flirt with others and will want to be the center of attention in his worth group. His behavior may even become so intolerable that you need to find your own way home . . . or worse yet, you are left to walk home alone in the dark. (Ask me how I know. Yes, my former spouse did this to me.) Holidays and special events are not off limits to the narcissist. As a matter of fact, the narcissist is known to be a destroyer of holidays and special occasions. My toxic former partner told me Easter Sunday before going to my cousin's house he was leaving me and had picked his married co-worker mistress. My former spouse sent a text message (a text message) to me telling me he filed for divorce (on our nearly 30-year marriage) a few hours before a major fundraising fashion show luncheon of which I was a member. (I couldn't believe it. I was blindsided by a text message and the timing of his cruelty yet again. He took the victim mentality of "I can't do anything right, can I?" Strategic and cruel. Nothing is off limits to the toxic individual.

Soulless – Does the narcissist really have a soul? I don't know. It sure seems like he is an evil entity who has no heart . . . sort of like Satan. Go no contact.

Soulmate – Because the narcissist is so attentive to you, asks about your hopes, dreams, desires, weakness, strengths, and so on, you will think you have found your soulmate. This is a very intense, intimate-feeling period. The narcissist will systematically begin making you feel worthless and fill you with self-doubt by withholding affection. The narcissist is not your soulmate. Once this toxic individual hurts your feelings, do not give him a second chance to do it again . . . because he will do it again, only worse. There are no reasons, explanations good enough to give this person your self-worth. Never do it again.

Snake – The narcissist is a sneaky venomous snake who slithers into your life. He will bite with those sharp fangs and will shoot poison in your eyes if he feels as though he's losing control, disrespected, or being attacked. Anytime you ask a question of the narcissist, he will feel attacked. (FYI—The narcissist always feels under attack. He will turn you into the enemy.)

Sneaky – The narcissist is sneaky. The narcissist is a sneaky snake. When you get that feeling, turn and run and go no contact.

Snide – The narcissist cannot carry on a disagreement in an adult or mature manner. The narcissist uses snide, mean, underhanded remarks to make you feel bad about yourself.

Special – The narcissist thinks he is special, has special abilities no one else has, and that you are fortunate that he "picked" you to be with. Picked you. He is the prize.

■ The narcissist will treat you as if you are special, wonderful, and will make you believe (in a short period of time) that you are his soulmate and he's been searching for someone just like you for so long. (He has been searching for someone like you . . . someone to make his victim.) You will have this fairytale feeling, but like all fairy tales, it is an illusion. This period of feeling special is short-lived once you submit to his charms. Then the abuse will begin.

Spin/Spin doctor/Spinner – If you think the news media can spin a story in any direction they want, well, they do not have nearly the skills a narcissist does. The narcissist will take bits and pieces of a conversation and turn it around. He will twist and turn, lie, manipulate the story. He will throw in trivial facts. He will blatantly create stories and distort facts to distract from the main point. He will lead you away from your point in a direction you had no idea that you were even heading. Your head will "spin" while he is doing it. You will wonder, "How did we arrive at this?" You, my friend, have been spun. You need to leave this person. It does not get better.

Spiteful – Condescending, rude, malicious, nasty words follow the dreamy, romantic love bombing.

Stalker – The narcissist wants to control you, who you are with, what you are doing, what you are saying. To control this, the narcissist needs to know what you are texting, reading, doing. The content of your life is the narcissist's obsession. The narcissist will stalk you in person, electronically, tracking your vehicle, hide in parking lots, wait for you at the grocery store, doctor's office, and at work. The narcissist may even demand to know almost word for word what it was you talked about with your sister or friend for two hours on the phone. (You better can recall it or else there will be an escalated problem.) Do not post where you are going, or where you are at on social media. If you feel the need, do so as you leave. Walk to your vehicle with someone and do not let that person leave until you look in the back seat. Change all your passwords frequently even if you do not think he has them. Cancel your credit cards and order new ones. Protect yourself!

Standards – The narcissist has extremely high standards and expectation in which you must meet or you will be chastised, compared to others who were able allegedly able to do what he wanted by meeting them thereby making you feel inferior.

■ The narcissist will accuse you of having extremely high standards that no one can meet. He will make you feel like you are "too much" for him because of your "impossible" standards and expectations; when, your standards and expectations are normal. The narcissist does not like that you have standards and expectations for yourself. He will criticize you telling you that your standards are too high and that no one can meet your impossible standards. The narcissist will try to make you feel bad about yourself. You need to have standards for yourself. The narcissist does not want you to have standards. He wants to control you.

Stares – The narcissist has a stare. You will notice it. I would explain it away in my mind. I think he is trying to figure out if you are buying his line of bull.

Stealth – The sneaky snake toxic abuser is clever in his destroying of your self-confidence and self-worth. The narcissist uses strategy to deteriorate your self-confidence and self-worth. When you are in bed on a beautiful sunny day sobbing wondering "what," "how," and "why" the answer is because you've become the victim of a toxic individual.

Stepping out of line – There will come a time when you are accused of stepping out of line. (Um, what line?) This means you are not obeying, or submitting, to the narcissist.

Stonewalls – The narcissist is evasive. The narcissist uses avoidance tactics. The narcissist will obstruct your progress in most areas. This is done to make you feel inferior and to create anxiety and worry. You know you can't ask the narcissist yet again for information for fear of being belittled. So, you choose to keep it inside and let the anxiety grow. If you cannot ask questions of the person with whom you are in a relationship without feeling worried and stressful most of the time, walk away from this. It will not get better.

Strategy – The narcissist is a master at strategy. Do not try to figure out the narcissist's strategy. Just walk away from this toxic person and his followers. You need to protect yourself by going no contact. Do not engage with his gaslighting, or with his provoke and blame tactics. Provoke and blame is intended to turn the tables on you to make you look like an aggressor, or overly angry. There are so many strategies the narcissist will employ. The narcissist will use your personal wounds and weaknesses to hurt and exploit you. He has planned your demise in several different ways with him coming out on top, or away from damage whatsoever. He will manipulate his followers and flying monkeys; making them believe he is the victim. Him. He is the victim. He will concoct stories about you that have no basis of reality. Walk away. Surround yourself with nurturing, supportive people.

Stress – The narcissist is always under stress and blames his bad behavior on his stress and problems, oh and blames the stress on you as well. You will feel stress most of the time when you are in a relationship with the narcissist. If the narcissist is feeling stress, the narcissist wants you to feel stress too. If the narcissist is not feeling stress, the narcissist wants you to feel stress and worry anyway. Nice person, huh? You will wonder where that super nice guy you used to be in a relationship went to. Let me tell you that he never really existed. He was an illusion. The narcissist is a wolf in sheep's clothing.

Stress on you – Unfortunately the anxiety and stress on you could possibly manifest in illness. You could develop a whole host of things due to the stress of the narcissist on your psyche, emotions, and actual well-being. If you notice you are going to the doctor for one thing after another, coupled with depression and anxiety, it is probably your toxic relationship penetrating your physical well-being. Of course, continue seeing the doctor. I would imagine as soon as you break free and cut the emotional cord from the toxicity of the draining narcissist, you will begin to heal and feel a world better.

Stringing along – The narcissist will string your emotions, your feelings, your plans along without making a commitment. The narcissist will use avoidance and breadcrumb.

Strings attached – The narcissist has strings attached to everything he does for you. Make no mistake, he didn't do it out of the goodness of his heart. It will come back to haunt you in one form or another, sometimes guilt, sometimes possessiveness, sometimes requiring a reciprocation of greater value.

Stuck – You will feel stuck while you are with the narcissist. You will feel stuck without the narcissist. It is a lonely, self-defeating feeling. You can get help to break through that stuck feeling. You are not stuck. It's a lie the narcissist implanted in your mind. A specialist will help you become empowered and help to heal you so you can move past this feeling.

Submissive – A submissive woman seems to be the narcissist's favorite type of woman. He has control over a submissive partner. The problem is, there is no challenge for the narcissist. He knows when he cheats on you, the submissive person will forgive him. He knows when he rips you off, the submissive person will forgive him. He knows he can lie to your face because the submissive partner will forgive him. Don't be submissive to anyone. It isn't empowering. It isn't cute.

Submit – The narcissist expects you to give in to his whim. The narcissist expects you to jump when he says jump . . . .and you better or he will turn the tables on you and create an issue, escalate the issue, blame you, leave you, give you the silent treatment, along with other punishments. Then after some time, when he feels like it or has used one of his other side chicks, will return to you to reclaim love. He will breadcrumb you.

Subversive – Should the narcissist feel that you, or anyone else, has crossed him, disrespected him, criticized him, questioned him, back talked him, the narcissist will cause problems and trouble for you, and anyone else, in a sneaky snake, behind the scenes manner. The narcissist will set you up to fail. The narcissist will seek to embarrass you. You might be gaslighted, baited, provoked, or several any of the other narcissist's favorite humiliation tactics. The narcissist is big into payback (even when it is not warranted because the action the narcissist is assigning to you didn't happen).

Success – The narcissist wants success at all costs. Only his success is important and should be celebrated. Your success may not even be acknowledged let alone celebrated or praised. The narcissist may even try to downplay your accomplishments so that he is able to feel superior. Any person, friend, family member, or relationship partner, who is not happy for you for your accomplishments are not necessary for your life. They are jealous and most likely toxic. Re-evaluate who is authentically supportive to you. The others can fade to black.

Suffocating – With the emotional terrorizing by the narcissist, and maybe the even physical invasion of your space by the narcissist, you may feel suffocated. If you try to talk to him about it, you are in for trouble. Perhaps you enjoyed the attention and love bombing (because you were unaware that you were being manipulated by a narcissist). Once the narcissist has you in his web, he will turn the tables on you and tell you that you are suffocating him. He's a jerk who is playing games with your mind and your heart. You need to leave now.

Suicide – Being in a relationship with a narcissist is toxic. The abuse and manipulation of your mind happen methodically and systematically making sure to use your weaknesses to make you spiral into the deep abyss. You will believe there is no way out of your relationship with this monster. The narcissist will manipulate you into thinking your life is worthless and pathetic and that your mere existence is too much for anyone to handle. The relationship with the narcissist could leave you on the brink of suicide. You are not alone. Even if you kept the belittling and abuse a secret from everyone you know, you are still not alone. Even if no one believes you that this super guy is not capable of the things you say he is, or that he's as gentle as a dove, you are not alone. This is the playbook of the narcissist and the narcissist's flying monkeys. Go no contact from the narcissist. What you need to do is to seek help from a qualified expert to help you regain your life.

Superior – The narcissist believes he is superior in all aspects: conversationally, academically, athletically, socially, religiously, career, monetarily or in a sacrificial manner, and so on. If someone is noted to be gifted or talented in an area, the narcissist will make fun of the person, or celebrity. This happens because the narcissist's extreme low self-esteem cannot handle anyone else getting positive attention (regardless if the narcissist knows the person or not).

Superman of love – Yes, that is right. He demands lovey-dovey nicknames. After he breaks your heart, you will feel foolish in remembering the names you lovingly gave him. He is not a superhero, regardless of what he believes about himself. He will not rescue your heart. On the contrary, he will destroy it.

Supply – The narcissist pulls his personality from other people. He is an inauthentic person who needs admiration from others to feel good about himself. He needs to make the target of his supply feel inferior to feel superior.

Support – The narcissist will remove you from people who offer you support. He will isolate you from the good people. He will make up and say disparaging things about people you care about and love. He will say they do not like him so he does not want to be around them. The things the narcissist declares may or may not be true, but the narcissist has no permission to isolate you from them . . . unless you give it to him.

Supportive people – Surround yourself with only supportive, nurturing people during your recovery. I cannot stress this enough. If you sense anyone does not have your best interest or shows you they do not have your best interest, or you find out someone is sabotaging your recovery with any type of unkindness: let them walk. You have been through hell. You do not have to stay there. This is your very important recovery time. There are so many good people out there who truly want you to succeed and want to help you through the darkness. I promise you, there is light at the other end of the tunnel.

Surrendering our power – Why in the world do we do this? The narcissist is a sneaky snake who belittles, degrades, shames, guilts, and so on with his manipulation tactics so we are tricked into proving our loyalty to him, giving him control of our emotions. There are weaknesses in each one of us. If we do not figure out our issues and make amends with them, we give others permission to exploit us as well. My suggestion is to work on reclaiming your power, self-worth with specialists and to go no contact with this toxic individual who will be a huge detriment and not at all supportive in self-improvement.

Suspicious – The narcissist is always suspicious of people, including you. At first, he will claim you are the only person he trusts. That is such an aphrodisiac. Being a person that someone else trusts gives (false) significance to your existence. He will indicate you are the "only" one he has ever trusted. Forget that line when the narcissist begins questioning you at length, turning everything you do and say into unseemly and uncouth actions you ultimately "wanted" to occur. It is bizarre and crazymaking. It is gaslighting. It is provoke and blame. It creates anxiety and worry and makes you question your subconscious motives unfavorably. (It goes that deep.) If someone is suspicious of you, why do you want to be with someone who is like this? I cannot stress enough to seek help in building up your self-worth and working on addressing weaknesses and wounds.

Switchbacks – Narcissists use this manipulation to confuse conversation, turn the tables on you, gaslight you, and provoke and blame you. It is like whiplash.

Symbiotic – Initially the narcissist provides the illusion that you are in a mutual-love, mutual-respect, mutually balanced relationship. As time goes on, this illusion crumbles and you will discover it is skewed to the side of the narcissist. You gave away your power so he could exploit you so this is going to happen. You need to seek help from a specialist to heal weaknesses and wounds. You will find empowerment by doing those things.

Sympathy – Regardless of what type of narcissist you are dealing with, the narcissist loves sympathy for his "struggles" with you, with the job, with family, with his life choices, with his upbringing . . . and on and on and on. The narcissist will blame any shortcomings on those things as well (providing he admits to shortcomings in the first place. They are not his fault nonetheless.) The narcissist will not give you authentic, real sympathy. If someone dies, "suck it up buttercup." Or, "how does it affect me?" Yes, these are things I have heard from the narcissist.

■ The narcissist does not have sympathy or compassion for you. He is exploiting you for heaven's sake. He finds you to be pathetic. Do not need help with a project because he is too busy to help you. Do not get sick because you will become an instant liability to him. If you are ill, the narcissist is annoyed and cannot be bothered. (Don't you realize what an inconvenience your illness/disability/disease is for him? Geez.) You are taking attention away from him when you are sick. Come on now, it better be all him all the time. Didn't you know that?

T

Taker – A narcissist is a taker. The narcissist takes your emotions, love, affection, time, money, activities, holidays, food, clothing, vehicle, phone, computer, tests, education, job, and so on. A narcissist will take them from you . . . and will use them to destroy you. Be careful though; you, after all, gave the narcissist these things. Stop allowing takers in your life by becoming more confident in who you truly are.

Talker – The extrovert narcissist talks a lot. The narcissist talks about things that primarily concern things he is interested in. He will try to persuade you to whatever it is he wants. The narcissist thinks his life, his issue is the most important topic there is. He is very self-absorbed and self-centered. The narcissist talks as though he is the most knowledgeable of all. When the narcissist is in the early stages of "winning you over," listen carefully. The narcissist will divulge who he really is. Turn and run and never look back. Never ever.

■ Conversely, the covert narcissist withholds conversation and instead uses looks and signals to communicate. This inability to speak with other people shows a lack of emotional development as this type of narcissist uses the most basic, rudimentary form of communication (like a baby or a caveperson).

Talks down – To make you feel stupid, or inferior, the narcissist will talk down to you with words, tone, and in a mocking manner. He is condescending to hurt you, shame you, and put you in your place. Like an immature child, he will even repeat things you say.

Tantrum – The narcissist uses pouting, growling, grunting, silent treatment, running away, storming off, walking off, walking ahead, yelling, screaming, throwing things, and destruction of property. All the same behaviors a two or three-year-old uses when throwing a temper tantrum. This is further proof that the narcissist is developmentally stunted.

Target – The narcissist will study the target/victim. The narcissist will prey on your weaknesses. Then will exploit them. You are nothing more than a challenge to see how far the narcissist can take it with you. Meanwhile, the narcissist is out running around, living is toxic life. Stop being a target of narcissistic abuse by getting help. Until you get help with recovery, you are likely to repeat being victimized by another narcissist, or the same narcissist. You need to get help.

Teasing – The narcissist will "joke" around with you disguised in a "playful" manner while undercutting you, degrading you, being intentionally cruel to you. When your feelings get hurt, the narcissist will tell you that you are hypersensitive, that he will "never" joke with you ever again because you can't take his humor (jerk). He will shame you for not wanting to be teased in a malicious way. (No one should be teased in a mean way. That is called bullying.)

Therapy – You need to get help from an expert to help in your recovery from narcissistic abuse.

■ A narcissist way he is willing to go to therapy. He won't go. The narcissist may even make the appointment and attend therapy. This is done to gather the psychological terminology to use against you. The narcissist will discontinue therapy after one or two . . . maybe even three times declaring there is nothing wrong with him. Even claiming the therapist said there is nothing wrong with him. RED FLAG! There is not one competent therapist, counselor, coach who is going to stop seeing someone who wants to self-improve. Remember that! A narcissist does not want to improve because the narcissist thinks he is fine . . . better than fine . . . as he is.

Thoughtless – The narcissist is thoughtless. The narcissist is punishing you or putting you in your place for reasons known only to him. He may be jealous of a success you had. Or he may be mad that you did not obey him and his absolute desires and needs. The narcissist knows you are waiting to hear from him, but he doesn't care about you. If you are upset because of his rude and/or inconsiderate behavior, the narcissist will let you know that it is your own fault in some twisted way. The best thing to do is to walk away and go no contact. The narcissist is a jerk who will never change or become self-aware. In fact, the boorish behaviors of the narcissist will only get worse. If you stay around for narcissistic abuse, this tactic will become transparent because you will see it happening so often. It is pathetic and immature; and, is a favorite of the narcissist.

Threatened – The narcissist is threatened by most everyone around him. He will claim he is not afraid of anyone or anything. He is. He is threatened by other's success, other's happiness, attention others receive. He will malign, put down, and backstab anyone and every one of whom he feels threatened (for no apparent reason). Threats are illegal. Document it and report it to a professional.

Threatening – The narcissist will both overtly and covertly threaten you. All aspects of your life, including your security, your future, your character, your reputation, your well-being, your safety, your family, your job, your finances, and so on will be threatened at one point or another the longer you stay in the relationship. The narcissist will threaten your safety, freedom, emotional and mental wellness, as well as your actual being. The abuser will then claim you are making too much out of what he did or said. You are too sensitive. You misunderstood. (Hint: oh no you didn't!) Leave anyone who threatens you in any way. This is an unsafe person!

Threats – The narcissist will threaten you to put you under his control. He is out of control so he uses threats. The threats may be outright or veiled. Threats are illegal. Tell an authority like the police, an attorney, a counselor, clergy, or family doctor. You need to have it documented by a professional. Of course, go no contact from this jerk.

Throwing stones – The narcissist will accuse you, and attempt to shame you into explaining yourself, for things of which he is guilty of doing/not doing. It's bizarre. He will use his contrived reasons why it is perfectly acceptable for his behavior but not for yours of the same thing. The phrase "don't throw stones if you live in a glass house" comes to mind when the narcissist is using this manipulation to make you feel inferior.

Time – The narcissist is vague on giving time he wants to meet you. The narcissist evades the question. The narcissist hates when you ask the question. The narcissist becomes annoyed by you, upset with you, may even turn the normal, innocent question into a huge rage or argument. The narcissist is always looking for something better. The narcissist is only concerned with his time and how it is used. The narcissist does not care that he is being inconsiderate to you by avoiding giving you a time . . . and then expects you to jump when he does text/call you with a time. Very inconsiderate. The narcissist doesn't care though. Throwing you off, making you feel bad, making you wonder is fun for the narcissist because he is making you feel inferior and putting you in your place.

■ Time – The narcissist has not evolved from a younger developmental time.

■ Time – The narcissist is rigid in his plans and in what he wants to do, in his routine. He will continue, taking care of him and his needs on his time frame.

■ Time – It takes time for the narcissist to come to the surface. When he does, don't question it or try to figure him out as you may be pulled in further, losing your own precious time. If someone is showing you who they are, you need to believe him. Get out of that toxic relationship.

Time switching – The narcissist will lie about times to meet. The narcissist will tell you one time, and show up another time (if at all). This is a psychological game to keep you guessing and on your toes. It will make you look as though you are needy when you begin to constantly double check the time. You are not needy. The narcissist is an immature game player and is treating you like the pawn. Sick of the crazymaking gaslighting? Get out of this relationship by going no contact.

Tolerate – The narcissist will make sure you learn how lucky, how fortunate, you are that he puts up with you and your nonsense. He will make sure you know he is tolerating your behavior, your incompetence, your drama, your . . . whatever, and you should feel grateful for it.

Tone – While the narcissist will deny using undercutting, or dismissive, tone with you, he will turn the tables on you and tell you that you are the one with an attitude or a tone in your voice that he doesn't like. This imaginary tone will be his righteous justification for creating arguments, pouting, getting mad at you, punishing you, and giving you the silent treatment. Your tone. Please . . . He is the one with the tone and the attitude.

Toxic – The narcissist, or person who is narcissist-like, is poisonous to you your emotional well-being. The narcissist will cause harm to your emotional well-being. The narcissist will cause your emotional well-being to deteriorate. The narcissist is a bully.

Tragic victim – Ohhhhhh boy oh boy. The narcissist is always a whining, complaining victim. Even his unlucky events are more serious, sad, and tragic than anything you have ever been through or will experience. (Oh brother. Ugh.)

Trauma – The narcissist will claim he suffered some sort of trauma as a child (and this may or may not be true). This so-called trauma will be the narcissist's self-proclaimed reason for all the woes, problems, and noticed bad behavior in his life. The unsavory behavior he has now is because of his childhood. Everyone has had something traumatic in their life. Normally-developed people seek help in healing and can overcome past experiences. The narcissist is unable to move past alleged trauma. This is the narcissist's excuse for everything. The narcissist expects sympathy for an event that may have happened 40 or 50 years ago. Seriously. When you notice this, and you bring it up to the narcissist, the narcissist will chastise you for not being empathetic to his childhood trauma.

■ The narcissist causes trauma in the victims or targets.

Traumatizer – The narcissist causes traumas, pain, fear, and anxiety to your emotional well-being.

Triangulation – The narcissist is a jealous, insensitive, insecure monster of a human being who will use a variety of games, tactics, methods, and pathology to instill those traits in another person (you—his victim). Triangulation is used to create jealousy and insecurity by the narcissist. Triangulation is when the narcissist uses a third person to instill fear, jealousy toward you as the primary partner to control you. This other person may be a woman ("best friend") at work, a judgmental family member (a mother or a sister), female friend. The third person is not going to support you. The third person is brought in to support the narcissist's overblown ego. If you are in a relationship with someone who brings in a third person in which intimate details of your relationship are shared and judged: leave! Run! Go no contact immediately! The narcissist is going to pounce and is using the third person to pick up steam and power.

Triggers – The narcissist is easily triggered. I cannot stress this enough. You do not know what will set off the narcissist. If you are late for dinner, the narcissist might shame you, impugn you as if you are a child. This may be harsh. It may even turn into an all-out punishment blast from the narcissist. The point is that the narcissist will be triggered by anything. Simple questions will be turned into lapses of judgment. Nice gifts will be turned into another one of your failures to please. You lovingly put your time, effort, concern, energy into making meals for the narcissist—who will complain how long it took to create for him, will complain how it doesn't taste like he wanted it to taste, and so on. Nothing is immune from a narcissist's trigger (not even the children and the pets).

■ While the narcissist has anger triggers, the narcissist will have implanted into your psyche fear triggers, as well as other types of control triggers to lower (or destroy) your self-esteem. You need help in recovering from this. Seek help from an expert.

Trivial – The narcissist wants you to "get over it" quickly. Get over what? Illnesses, surgery, sadness, depression, grief, shock, the death of a loved one, his cruel behavior. My former husband forced me to return to work the day after the funeral for my beloved best friend of over forty years, who was a member of my immediate family and was closer than a sister. He was incensed I was in shock over her death. He was annoyed I had a difficult time functioning after this person I spoke to many times a day had died. Needing a hysterectomy was an inconvenience to him and he let me know it every day. My former husband told me at the beginning of April he was leaving me. He told me he was going to "give me" until the end of June to get over it. He was so arrogant he told others this as well. This was brought up by my attorney. (As I was sitting in my attorney's office sobbing with PTSD, my attorney mentioned he said I had agreed to "get over it in two months. She then commented on his arrogance and promised to make him pay.) If it doesn't concern him, it isn't important (to him); and is, therefore "trivial." He will put on an act in public; but, in private he will show you how unimportant your needs, emotions, and feelings are to him.

Trust – Narcissists convinces the other person they are dysfunctional to the point the other person no longer can trust in their decisions, choices, and behaviors.

■ The narcissist does not truly trust anyone. The narcissist does not trust you.

■ Come on, admit it. You do not trust him. You are in anxiety and panic mode because you are afraid he is going to find someone else. He has instilled this fear in you. Why in the world do you want to be with someone you do not trust? (Here is the answer: You broke your boundaries. You gave him your power. He is destroying your self-worth. You do not trust him. Without trust, there is not love. He does not love you. You do not truly love him. Stop this nonsense! You need trust in a relationship and there is very little to none. That is not good enough!)

Truth – The narcissist is dishonest. The narcissist will lie even when the truth will suffice. The truth will bend the truth instead of being honest. The narcissist will insist you are wrong and he is right. He will use various levels of emotion, from calm to disgust to anger, when you do not believe the lie he is throwing at you. He will even take events you were at, situations you were in, and words/sentences you have said, twist them around and tell you what happened or was said in the narcissist own defense. It will leave you confused and baffled. Beware! This may be when the narcissist amps up his efforts into a full-blown opportunity to bait and bash you. When you notice the pattern of lies, do not bother trying to "talk about it" with the narcissist because he is not a rational being. It is pointless. Anything YOU say WILL be used against you. Instead, go no contact. The narcissist is toxic.

Turning the tables (on you/or others) – The narcissist will not take responsibility for most anything. The narcissist will turn the tables on you, blame shift, blame you, bash and blame, bait and blame. You will be accused of the most bizarre things when all you wanted to do was bring up something that is bothering you.

Two faced – The narcissist is a hypocrite, insincere, a liar, and cannot be trusted. The narcissist will tell you one thing and will do or say another thing. The narcissist will lie to your face, and behind your back.

U

Ulterior motives – The narcissist has an agenda of his own. The reason his agenda includes you is for a benefit to him only. It is most definitely to boost his ego. The many secondary motives are varied and are according to his needs, wants, and what he can get/take from you.

Ultimatums – The narcissist will issue demands and expect you to follow them. It really doesn't matter because the narcissist will find fault with you. While he will dole out directives, he does not want to hear from you. He will turn most of your needs into "ultimatums." He will perceive normal conversations as ultimatums, or turn normal conversations into ultimatums, and will likely flip out on you.

Unapologetic – Any apology you may receive from the narcissist is insincere, or attached to an agenda. Most likely you will receive a non-apology or will give a half-hearted apology and will add a "but . . ." followed with blame and turning the tables on you. I've heard so often how I was the cause of his behaviors and his choices. He would say, "You made me do it." Me? I wasn't in the room, the location, or even the same town; but still, it was somehow my fault.

Unavailable – The narcissist is unavailable to you on several levels. The narcissist is unavailable to you emotionally. The narcissist is unavailable often when you want/need him in person. The narcissist is unavailable to provide various types of support to you. Let's face it, the narcissist is not available to be in a healthy, balanced relationship with you. Stop trying to make a square peg fit into a circle hole.

Unaware – The narcissist doesn't do the internal work to become self-aware. The narcissist is unaware of your needs, wants, desires, hopes because he does not care about your things important to you.

Uncompromising – The narcissist wants his way. All the time. He is not open for negotiations. It's his way or the highway. (Don't be surprised when he admits it arrogantly.)

Under attack – The narcissist can criticize, demean, shame, and belittle you on most any given topic. You will feel under attack for your career, your relationships, your choices, and your decisions. The narcissist does this to you because he is internally attacking most everything about himself. The narcissist's self-loathing is not your problem so don't take on a project of trying to fix him. You cannot fix him. You need to fix yourself by figuring out why you want to stay with an abuser. (Hint: The work you do for yourself is hard, but it is so worth it. The work you do in healing past wounds and hurts will change your life in amazing ways.)

Undercutting – The narcissist will find slight ways to make you feel bad, to make you feel inferior, and to question yourself. It's an almost constant part of his personality. Should you address his remarks with him, you will be made a fool. He will say he was just joking and that you are overdramatic. You are taking it the wrong way. (Riiiiiight.) He may even deny he ever said it . . . but you know he did. You know he said it. This guy is going to keep doing this to you.

Underestimate – Do not explain away the actions of a narcissist, or make excuses for them. Do not underestimate the narcissist's mean, controlling, destructive nature—against you. (You will innocently believe, "He loves/loved me. He would never do *that* to me.") The narcissist will be so bold as to tell you not to worry, he would never do that to you. BE AFRAID! He's giving you a hidden warning.

Underling – The narcissist takes advantage, exploits, abuses, and will end up being mean to anyone he feels is an "underling." An underling, in the narcissist's point of view, is anyone not as good as him and lower in some status. Of course, you are not his equal. You are an underling. Wait staff, service industry people are underlings. He can be rather condescending and even rude to waiters and waitresses. When you observe this behavior, know that it is beyond just being rude. He is showing you who he is. He is showing you how he treats people. He is showing you that he is a narcissist.

Undermine – The narcissist will overtly and covertly try to undermine your efforts in activities, goals, relationships, physical appearance, financial strength, and emotional well-being. Should you notice unkind murmurs by the narcissist, you are not misunderstanding him. He is trying to plant seeds of doubt and seeds of negativity in your mind.

Undetectable – Initially you will not know you are dealing with a narcissist. You will think this guy is your perfect partner . . . your soulmate. You will get little clues here and there, but will use denial, or will explain them away. Eventually, the little clues begin to increase and increase and increase. It is like boiling a frog. The poor little frog does not know he is being boiled to death because his body temperature increases as the heat is slowly increased in the pot . . . until he is no longer. It is slow and methodical.

Unethical – Look below the surface. The narcissist is without principles, is dishonorable, sneaky, a chronic liar, cheater, financial abuser, controller, manipulator. The narcissist is a hypocrite, projector, blame shifter, and so on. (You know what I am saying. I know you do.) The narcissist will trick you into defending or proving your ethics, standards, and expectations, all the while belittling you about them making you question yourself. The narcissist is grooming you for anxiety, worry, and to dominate and control you. If you see unethical behavior, leave the relationship. It's not a healthy one.

Ungrateful – The narcissist expects you to provide what he wants emotionally, financially, physically, and so on. The narcissist is not grateful for these things, even if you had to sacrifice something to provide it. The narcissist may say, "thank you" to you; but try to gauge if it is sincere or empty. Notice if there is true happiness in what it is you have given or provided; or, is the narcissist looking for something wrong—something about which he complains; something in which he can make you feel inferior or stupid. If this is a shared, group, or public activity, the narcissist may not even acknowledge your participation in it thereby showing you lacked worth in remembering your contribution. Your contribution may have been the guiding force, but the narcissist wants to put you in your place in making you feel inferior any way he can.

Unempathetic – Do you want to be in a relationship with someone who is caring, loving, sympathy when appropriate, understanding, appropriately sensitive, nurturing, attentive beyond the "love bombing" stage? Find someone else because the narcissist is none of these in the long run. He will hook you by appearing to have the wonderful qualities you want. He is the opposite. He is empty.

Unhealthy – Your inner voice is giving your signals, red flag warnings, and screaming at you that this person is unhealthy not just for you, but an overall emotionally unhealthy individual. The relationship with a toxic person will be unbalanced and not nurturing. It is dysfunctional. You know this because your inner voice IS telling you. LISTEN to your inner voice, stop making excuses and get out of this terrible dynamic. You deserve better.

Uninterested – Does the narcissist complain that you talk too much? Does he make you feel as you talk too much? He is uninterested. He is interested only as to how he can manipulate the information you are providing. Other than that, he doesn't care. He is uninterested at family, friend, and work events if he is not the center of attention. Is there a sporting event on tv? Yes, he's more interested in that than you or your family, friends, events. (He may even step out on your wedding reception to go watch the game, or to hang out with his friends.)

Unique – While we are all special and unique in our own ways, the narcissist takes this to an extreme belief. All the narcissist's struggles are unique, never experienced by anyone else ever. No one "understands" the narcissist's unique struggles. This lack of "understanding" of the narcissist's unique struggles will be thrown in your face and used against you to elicit a panic and worry that you are not being "good enough" for him. Girl, please. We all have issues. His problems are not so unique that you need to put yourself on the backburner ALL THE TIME. A balanced relationship isn't demanding that you pay attention only to his struggles and needs.

Unpredictable – You have no clue when the narcissist is going to flip out, or become annoyed with you, or even give you silent treatment punishments. The narcissist's unpredictable behavior is meant to keep you in the dark to who he really is: a toxic jerk! Instead, being a nurturer that you are, you will probably internalize what is going on to try to figure out what happened, and how to make it better. The narcissist's unpredictability is intended to keep you on edge leaving you worrying, filled with anxiety, and chipping away at your self-worth. His unpredictable behavior is on him . . . it's not your issue. Leave this clown. You deserve better. Do not give him any extra chances to damage you. Go no contact and don't look back.

Unreasonable – The narcissist is unreasonable in his demands and expects you to follow them. If you question anything, you are picky, unreasonable, paranoid, needy, overly sensitive, crazy . . . and the list goes on.

Unreliable – The narcissist is unreliable by design. The narcissist does not care about you, your expectations or standards. The narcissist does not care about your needs or wants. The narcissist will continually let you down, disappoint you, hurt you, and break your heart. If you want to talk about your feelings, the narcissist will make you feel bad about your feelings and will turn things around on you, deflecting the situation and/or conversation.

Unstable – The narcissist is unstable. You don't know what he is going to do next, or why, or if you will get in trouble for it. This causes a great deal of worry.

Unwilling to admit fault – It's bizarre how he twists things around, blame you, and you end up apologizing for his misdeed . . . most likely because, if all other reasons fail, "you made him do it."

Unwritten rules – There are so many rules the narcissist imposes on you. These rules, ridiculous as they are, are constantly changing. This is meant to throw you off, self-question yourself, and to give the narcissist a reason to demean and belittle you.

Unyielding – Once the narcissist finds something that will give him attention (regardless if it is negative or positive attention), the narcissist will hold onto a "belief" if it suits his needs. This closed-minded behavior could go on for decades.

User – The narcissist is a user. The narcissist will take anything you have to offer without giving anything back in return. The narcissist will use your abilities, position in a job/society, love, intelligence, reputation, finances, and so on. The narcissist will even expect to take things from you that you don't even have. The narcissist will expect you to somehow get them or make them available for him or for his use . . . even to your detriment. Do not do it. Have some self-respect and disregard the unpleasantness coming your way of what he thinks and says about your refusal to be his pathetic puppet. You are empowered! Show him how empowered you are as you walk out of the door!

V

Vague – The narcissist does not give direct answers to you. The narcissist will give you demands and orders. You are sure you have followed the demands. Even then, the narcissist will have changed the demands and you didn't know. The narcissist is vague. The narcissist will make sure to be unclear with plans, direction, and even with things about the narcissist himself. The narcissist does not truly know who he is; therefore, the narcissist is as vague as possible. Later the narcissist can criticize you for "getting it wrong." Both the covert and overt narcissists are very clever with this manipulation.

Vain – Regardless if you are in a relationship with a covert, overt, or extrovert type of narcissist, how things appear to others, more importantly how he appears to others, is of primary importance. The narcissist does not know how to live an authentic life. The narcissist is a fake. The narcissistic mask is not necessarily about the vanity of conceit. Narcissism goes much deeper and further beyond that.

Validation – A narcissist needs constant validation for everything he does (regardless of how mundane, required, or even participatory it is). If you forget or neglect to give him the validation he requires, you are in for it. The narcissist will turn this into a big issue of you not being grateful; or, how much you don't care about him. It's immature. It's insecure. It's his issue, not yours. Don't fall into this trap.

Value – In most healthy relationships, there is a desire to make the other person feel special. The partners care about each other. In a relationship with the narcissist, the narcissist values his needs, his wants, and his desires above all others to the point of lying to weasel out of being with you. You may have had a huge accomplishment, but the narcissist would prefer being at home watching sports. You are not a priority. You will end up being alone in your car, eating a slice of pizza as a celebration. That's how little the narcissist cares. If you try to share your feelings with him, he will be incensed and/or enraged because you are not caring about HIS needs. Of course, he will spin it to make you feel shame and guilt with lines like, "what did I do wrong now?" Or, "it is never enough with you." Nice, right? Meanwhile, you just achieved the goal of a lifetime. Instead of having presents and happiness, you have tears running down your face and his immature and boorish silent treatment. (You better end the call before the commercial on the sporting event ends or else you will be accused of trying to force the narcissist to miss some of the event. But wait, what about that important accomplishment? It magically became a non-issue when the narcissist changed the focus. Slick very slick.) Know this: in a relationship with a toxic person like a narcissist, you are always alone . . . even if he is right there beside you.

Value system – The narcissist mimics the value system of the person he is trying to charm. That value system will go out the window when he has his victim under his control and will use those values against the victim to demean and belittle the victim to maintain control.

Vengeance – The paranoia of the narcissist is that everyone is out to get him. Because of this belief, the narcissist is going to get revenge against his wrongdoers in some fashion. The covert narcissist is especially sneaky and clever with a vengeance.

Verbal con – Narcissists lie to confuse you. The narcissist uses diversion tactics to control you. The narcissist uses verbal cons from the first meeting, with the love bombing stage, and all throughout the relationship. The narcissist wants to seep into your emotions and into your mind to control you. Verbal cons are the method.

Verbal abuse – The abuser will hurt you mentally and emotionally with words, screaming, tone, belittling, and volume. The abuser wants you under control. The abuser will call you mean. The abuser will also call you mean and cruel names. He will say whatever bizarre and untrue statement he can think of to make you feel bad and to make you defend yourself, or prove your self-worth. It's a gaslighting technique.

Victim – The narcissist is always a victim. The narcissist lives in victim mentality. The narcissist looks at problems, complains, and is the victim. The narcissist takes the world outlook as if things are done on purpose to him like everyone is out to get him. You are a victim of the narcissist. When you feel sad about something, you are taking attention away from the narcissist. The narcissist does not care about anything that has happened to you. If there is any type of listening by the narcissist, it is so the narcissist can use what happened against you to lower your self-esteem. The narcissist will further instigate you . . . bait you . . . into a reaction. The narcissist has you where he wants you. He will then bash your response or behavior in reaction to the event that has made you sad, or have an unpleasant reaction. The narcissist will also make fun of you for being a victim by ridiculing you often saying things like "you're such a victim. You're always a victim." in a derogatory manner. Instead of talking with you and elevating you, the narcissist will use this as an opportunity to shame and hurt you.

Victim mentality – He will complain, whine, get angry, and jealous of trivial issues and other people endlessly. He takes on the victim mode when he must be all thing to everyone . . . or so he believes and behaves, and of course tells everyone. These are self-imposed problems that can be avoided. The narcissist does not practice being proactive or tackling things head-on. He prefers to wait until little problems are mountains. The narcissist will escalate most everything quickly from a non-issue to a huge problem, or to a rage. The narcissist does not want to avoid problems. He wants to make problems worse and be totally embroiled in the drama of them. He thinks he will gain sympathy and attention by having these problems. The narcissist has more medical issues than I can count. Migraines: you bet. It must be taxing in the mind of the narcissist always plotting and strategizing.

Victimhood – The narcissist blames others for his own problems. He could do something about them, but chooses not to make a change (because it is, after all, never his fault . . . so he believes). He would rather complain and blame than figure out how to improve whatever his problem is. He is such a victim. (Eye roll.)

Victimization – The narcissist is a victim. The world is out to get him. The narcissist uses lies, manipulations, and projections to take on his victimization. The narcissist can get both negative and positive attention from being a victim. Attention is key for the narcissist. The victimization he claims as his own. He has a victim mentality and expects pity from you, allegiance and loyalty. The narcissist will then use these things to control you as you are an empathetic person. See, he has already tested you and gained your trust. The victimized narcissist uses a great deal of blame in his repertoire. The narcissist is poor: it's someone else's fault. The narcissist didn't get the job: it's someone else's fault. The narcissist is sick: there is a never-ending slew of sicknesses to fuel the attention seeking. The victimized narcissist always has some problem that is someone else's fault. You will help the narcissist over and over and over . . . .it is never-ending. There is always something—some sort of crisis, medical issue, or drama.

Vindictive – If the narcissist thinks you have done something wrong (even if you haven't done anything—the narcissist is paranoid), something that makes the narcissist upset or angry, you better believe forgiveness is not on the table. The narcissist will wait, torment you over this "sin" against him, or undesirable act and then do something mean and vindictive to "put you in your place" so he can show you who is boss. Even if you ask permission (asking permission is expected) to do something, the narcissist will be angry you are not sitting at home pining over him. You were having fun. Shame will be waiting for you. You will be punished in some manner. Make no mistake about it. It will only increase in severity as time goes on. You should leave this relationship as soon as possible and go no contact. The narcissist is twisted and will seek to hurt you.

Violence – The violence in a narcissistic relationship is emotional. It can be physical, as well as verbal. You must seek help to recover from narcissistic abuse syndrome.

Vulnerable – The longer you are involved with the toxic person, the more power you will be tricked into giving away to him. By giving away your power, you will become vulnerable to his cruel manipulative emotional abuse. The opposite of vulnerable is empowered. To be empowered, you need to regain your self-worth. You can only do that by not having someone in your life who chips away at your psyche.

Vulnerable narcissist (also known as an introverted narcissist, covert narcissist, hypersensitive narcissist, closet narcissist) – like the overt/grandiose narcissist, the vulnerable narcissist also has a sense of entitlement, grandiose self-view, lacks reliability, exploits, manipulates, and uses deceit. The vulnerable narcissist is just as manipulative, sneaky, and underhanded as an overt narcissist.

W

Weak – The narcissist may be one of the most powerful people in the company, even in the world. That does not matter. The narcissist is a weak, pathetic, deeply damaged human being. The narcissist thrives by hurting, humiliating, and emotionally destroying another person through narcissistic abuse. That is one weak human being. Turn and run and go no contact.

Web of lies – The narcissist will involve you in his lies or cover-ups. He will use that type of behavior to then turn the tables on you and call your character into question for defending him. The narcissist might also blackmail you blackmail you with the things you did for him. He will use revenge on you and threaten you. Anyone who wants to hurt you like this is not safe for you, nor is he worth your time. Just walk away from this creep and go no contact. If you need to involve the police, don't hesitate.

Whiner – Regardless if your narcissist is a vulnerable narcissist or a grandiose narcissist, whining is involved. It usually occurs before the rage stage.

Winner – The narcissist's objective is to win his agenda at all costs. He has a "me versus you" mentality. That may even include a simple game of cards. Should the narcissist lose, a deafening pouting with aggression will follow. The narcissist is not a good sport.

Worry – The narcissist causes worry in his victims. If you are feeling worried about your interaction with your narcissist, you need to seek help right now. Healthy, loving, supportive relationships do not trigger worry, panic, and/or fear. Go no contact from this person immediately.

Wounded – The narcissist claims to be damaged or wounded in some way. The narcissist uses his childhood abuse, or the no one understands his story to work on the empath. If you believe his sad tale (which could quite possibly be true), know this: His damage and his wounds are not yours to fix, understand, or help him work through. You cannot fix him. All humans have varying levels of pain. Your pain is no less than his. The difference between the narcissist having pain and you having pain is that he does not care that you have wounds or pains.

Wounds – The narcissist will prey on your weaknesses and your emotional wounds. The emotional wounds on your psyche created by the narcissist are deep, with many levels and offshoots. Regardless of how long you are with the narcissist, you will be left with wounds. Get help for recovery.

■ Some wounds are physical. Take pictures. Call the police. Go to the hospital. You need to follow through with pressing charges and holding the narcissist accountable. If you don't, the narcissist will turn everything around on you to attempt to make you look like you are the abusive one. Gaslighting at its finest. Get out of this dangerous and toxic relationship. The narcissist does not love you so stop making excuses for him.

Wrongdoings – The narcissist will blame you for everything that goes on with him that looks like a negativity. If he cheats, it is your fault for not being good enough, or because you hurt his feelings, or you weren't paying enough attention to him, or you did something to drive him away to be with another person. You pushed him into it. If you are the other woman, God help you. The narcissist will likely blame you for having an affair and for manipulating and seducing him. Bottom line: he cheated! Will he apologize? Maybe. Will it be sincere? No, the apology will not be sincere. He will cheat again. Other wrongdoings are your fault too. He will blame you for tricking/manipulating him.

X

X – He's an ex so go no contact. Mark an "x" over his number. Delete his pictures, and block his number. Save the text and email messages because you may need to use produce these items for the authorities. Print them, and place them in a box for easy access.

■ Change your email address, phone number, and all passwords (even if you do not think he has them—change them to be on the safe side). Cancel your credit cards and order new ones. You may think I am suggesting too much. Make no mistake, the abuser wants to destroy you and wants to win at whatever cost there is. I gave my credit card to my attorney during the divorce so when my former husband ran up nearly $10K in a few short months, I was covered. I did not do it. I had nothing to do with those charges. The proof of who he is was in the pudding.

Y

You are not alone – Reach out. Friends are ready to help you. I'm sure they see who he really is too. Anyone who is not supportive, you need to forgive them and release them. I promise you, the good people you need in your life will appear. Share your story. You are not alone. I am here for you.

Grasping to Youth – Wonder why older people are with people noticeably younger than themselves? It is emotional immaturity. The young one is with the emotionally immature person for their own twisted issues. If the narcissist throws your age in your face, let this be a red flag to you of the narcissist's immature emotional development.

Z

Zeal – You had a zest for life. You will find it again when you are no longer with the narcissist. You will be able to do things that even surprise yourself! You will be amazing! Seek help to improve your self-esteem, practice forgiveness, and move on. Never look back at that jerk. Certainly, do not engage with him for any reason whatsoever. You will make it through recovery. It can be challenging and there may be tears; but with help, you will make it through the dark tunnel to the other side. Many people want to see you succeed. Anyone who does not wish you well, should not be in your circle of support or on your mind. Focus on only the good people. Focus on all your good qualities. I am pulling for you! I look forward to hearing your story of recovery and all the awesome things you WILL do with your new positive life without the weight of negativity the narcissist placed on you. With positivity in your life, YOU WILL SOAR!

WHY DOES THE VICTIM STAY
WITH THE ABUSER?

Ok, so I'll answer the insensitive question.

This is my perspective; my experience. This is how I felt, and what I went through. I imagine most victims of narcissist abuse feel the same way.

■ The victim's self-esteem is already fragile in some way when the narcissist enters the picture. A person with some sort of low self-esteem is fodder to the narcissist. I met him at age 17. At that time, I thought I was confident. I thought I knew what I needed to know at that point. I was not one of those, "I know it all" people. I knew I didn't. My husband was so intelligent and handsome. He knew more than me . . . or so he made me feel and believe.

■ Being systematically and strategically conditioned, or brainwashed, into believing most everything is the victim's fault, we don't believe anyone else will love us. We are taught that we should be "lucky" he, the narcissist, puts up with us. He is a saint for doing so. He is compared to being as gentle as a dove, and we, the victims, are the monster. It is a flip-flop bizarro world. This occurs mostly through verbal and emotional abuse. In my former relationship, physical abuse was also thrown into the mix. His abuse, however, was always "my" fault. I "made" him do it. It was something I did or said. I needed to do better, be better.

■ The narcissist or abusive partner tricks you into believing you need to constantly prove yourself. The abuser makes you feel worthless. While you are busy trying to prove yourself to your abusive partner, the abuser makes you believe that no one would put up with you, your stupidity, (and so on) because you're such a handful. You spend your relationship doing just that: trying to prove yourself, to prove your worth, to him. Then you beg the abuser to stay, to pick you because you just want "to do better" and sees that you do have value.

■ When you are in an abusive relationship, you go into denial. I did. I did not want to acknowledge that this person, who I loved, was abusing me. (I did not want to be one of "those" people.) And I certainly could not admit that I was "allowing" it. Victims are taught to accept the blame, but we would not "allow" someone to abuse or purposefully hurt us. Right?

After I had attempted suicide, was no longer with him, and was in recovery, there was no other way to describe how I felt (and why I stayed) as, "I was a boiled frog."

Below is a portion taken from "Soaring Minds Workbook and Journal." It is my Facebook post that shares why I stayed.

"My family doctor gave me the first tools to choose empowerment over suicide . . .

Facebook
May 9, 2015 post:
My doctor said to share my story. So, with great pain and angst, along with a whole host of emotion, here I go:

"#whyistayed

My husband, who I've known for 31 years (I met him as a teen), abused me once or twice a year for 31 years. He always apologized to me. I thought the love was more important to my heart than his fist to my stomach and back, or hands on my face, arms, legs, or his undercutting words. If it wasn't me he was hitting, he was putting a hole in the walls, and doors. I thought he would love me like no other and protect me from the world. He did everything for me. I mistook the absolute control over me, and of me, as love and guidance. He showed his love by providing a wonderful home and lifestyle, presents, clothing, and jewelry. I was grateful for everything he did for me.

I thought no one else would ever love me, want me, or want to put up with me. Everyone thought he was a saint . . . so did I.

He had an affair with a married co-worker with whom he works closely. He picked her over me. Then he changed his mind and picked me . . . then her . . . then me . . . and Easter morning, he picked her. That night was brutal. He beat me six times since 2015 began—the most times of any year previously. One time was so bad, I decided I could no longer take the abuse, his affair, the darkness of everything and all the secrets—I couldn't see tomorrow. My life was not as sparkly as I had pretended it to be. I decided "to be with Chris."

He apologized as was usual. I forgave him, as was usual for us—I believed his apologies which was usually accompanied by presents and many kindnesses—maybe they were to ensure the secrets, maybe he was sorry, maybe it was to fuel the illusion I helped create. I don't know.

The verbal abuse has been just as bad, maybe even worse.

For 31 years I kept the secret of abuse. I loved him. I protected him and his (what I thought) was his one flaw.

In reality, he didn't protect me though. He destroyed me. Because he had absolute control over me, I knew nothing about finances, did not trust my own decision making, and lost my confidence and lost who I was / who I am somewhere in the last 31 years. I lost me.

I thought I was loved.

I thought I was protected.

It was an illusion—just like when I put makeup on my black and blue legs and arms to cover the bruising: it was an illusion.

He emptied the bank accounts and left 19 cents in our checking. He controlled our finances. I did not know the name of our bank until he had to disclose it.

I depended on him for everything I thought he was taking care of me . . . it was his control over me.

He has a new go go go lifestyle.

He has a married coworker woman still with her husband,

He exercises nonstop pumping his ego along with the weights. He spends time at happy hour where fun times continue with coworkers and spouses are forbidden. He's a silent drinker who isn't so happy when he comes home. I learned to pretend I was asleep.

I thought I loved my life. Now, as healing begins, I realize the fear I loved in . . . and I thought it was happiness.

I don't know who he is.

I think I very well never truly have known him as I have learned, one of my best self-preservation mechanisms and self-protection is denial.

Denial brought me this far but did not do me any favors.

Neither did he . . .

This is my story of "why I stayed." Through therapy, I have learned (an am learning) about my denial, rose-colored glasses, my Disney-like version of happiness, and how a real man does and does not treat a woman.

I told my story. I didn't think anyone would really care. I didn't even reread it or proof it. I took a deep breath, hit the "post" button. I got up from the brown leather chair that morning, tossed the iPhone on the bed, and went to the kitchen. An hour or so I returned to my phone, turned it on and clicked on Facebook. I was stunned at the number of likes I had received on a Saturday morning in an hour. The comments equaled the likes, and the private messages I was receiving were in the tens. I sat down and began to read them all . . . tears filled my eyes as I read the stories of others. Tears of gratitude from the compassionate messages streamed down my face. The private messages contained messages of "thank you for posting" messages, messages telling me I am brave, messages of compassion, messages in which the sender related his /her emotion-filled, heartfelt story of abuse to me . . . with a thank you.

Sharing my story was empowering. Had the doctor not encouraged me to share it, I would have kept the torturous story that led me to suicide in the darkness of my mind. I wouldn't have been able to heal or recover. I wouldn't have learned so much about myself. I wouldn't have learned about my inner voice. I wouldn't have learned WHY I allowed him to have so much control over me. I want to encourage you to share your story. Speak it! Let it out! It's a freeing thing to do. The abuse does not have control over you when you talk about it. The "shame" of not being the perfect wife or the best couple melted away. I put a light directly on the problems instead of hiding the issues and abuses in the dark . . . like he wanted and like I was conditioned to do. For 30 years I wanted my friends and family to love him as I did. The thing is, he didn't love me or us. He used all of us. It was in sharing of my story that so many things became illuminated." (Hoffer, Michelle, 2017)

WHEN YOU LEAVE THE ABUSER

Use this a basic checklist toward your self-protection and healing.

■ Accept the fact that the narcissist never loved you. He didn't. He will never truly love anyone. Not the next one, not the one after that. He is incapable of authentic love with anyone. His world is all make-believe.

■ Go no contact.

■ Be proactive and protective of your safety. Do not go places alone. Do not walk to your car alone. Make sure to check the back seat before getting in the car and thanking someone for escorting you to the car.

■ Be proactive about your privacy rights.

■ HIPAA – Health Insurance Portability and Accountability Act. HIPPA protects your medical information privacy. You must make sure to change your "in case of emergency" by removing his name from medical records, gyms, dentist, eye doctor, medical, psychological, pharmacy, chiropractor, spas . . . anywhere you write an "in case of emergency" name. If you do not, he will have access to all your appointments, and medical information.

■ Change all your passwords—all of them.

■ Change the locks at your home—all of them.

■ Change your coming and going patterns.

■ Call the credit card companies, have new cards issued.

■ Call the bank, change your access information and inform them of what is going on.

■ You will go through the five stages of grief: denial, anger, bargaining, depression, and acceptance. It is hard; but there is light, and empowerment, at the other end of the tunnel.

■ Hold tight onto your goal of healing. Don't give in. Don't engage with him for any reason.

■ Surround yourself with only supportive, nurturing people during your recovery. I cannot stress this enough. If you sense anyone does not have your best interest or shows you they do not have your best interest, or you find out someone is sabotaging your recovery with any type of unkindness: let them walk.

■ Contact a specialist to set up an appointment to become a client. You need to improve your self-worth, understand the manipulations that occurred, learn how to forgive, and learn to love yourself.

■ Monkey mind of negative chatter amps up in your head. Meditate through it. Contact your supportive group of friends and family.

■ The narcissist may become seriously and dangerously obsessed with you. This could go on for weeks, months or years; or until he has a new side piece. There is no time limit on what he will do. It is imperative you do not give in to temptation in replying to his crazymaking and manipulations.

■ Become determined in your self-improvement and healing.

■ You'll cry. It's okay. You've been through a lot and you need time to process the damage the abuser created in your life. You need time to regain your self-worth. You need to de-program his toxic implanted messages.

■ Remember the first sentence on this page, "Accept the fact that the narcissist never loved you." (This is important in your recovery.)

#abusersabuse

NATIONAL DOMESTIC ABUSE HOTLINE
1-800-799-7233

A SECTION ON HEALING

Need help figuring out where to start? First, change all your passwords, call the bank and credit cards, and seek help from a specialist. Next, work on these things:

■ Acceptance – Accept yourself first and foremost. You're awesome! You must also accept that he never loved you. Never. He doesn't love anyone. He is incapable of love. It's his false mask. He wore it with you, and with everyone (even with his new target).

■ Ambitious – You can handle anything you want to do! Let nothing stand in your way! You survived the hell of a toxic individual; you can do anything!

■ Authentic – Listen to your inner voice and your intuition. Avoid people pleasing. This is YOUR time. Please YOU!

■ Automatic thoughts – You may hear his negative words in your head, and they may seem true. Seek help in getting rid of the monkey mind. Replace them with positive affirmations.

■ Be deliberate

■ Believe in yourself!

■ Boundaries – Set boundaries and keep them. If you don't want to do something, do not do it!

■ Build positive connections – People will leave your life. Don't hold onto to them. New people who are supportive, positive, beacons of goodness will surface and appear. Those are the ones to cherish. If you must prove yourself to anyone, they are not for you.

■ Call for love – When someone has wronged you, instead of getting upset, mad, or angry at them, shift that energy! Give people who are unkind a quick energy burst of love. They obviously need it; and shifting into a call for love for this person will keep you elevated, rather than drag you down. (It will also energetically help them, too, which is fantastic.)

■ Challenges – There will be times you feel like throwing in the towel or giving up on your goals or even yourself. Don't do it. Seek help to realign and get back on track. You will cry. It's okay. Call your supportive friends and family to tell them how you are feeling. (My cousin showed up with a white cake with white icing and stayed with me until I was calm and reset. She saved my life that day.)

- Coming out of the fog – This is a metaphor that seems to go be an often used one when recovering from abuse. It is how I felt when learning to live again. It was scary but so uplifting.

- Commit to positivity, joy, happiness, success

- Creativity – Engage your creativity in crafting, fine arts, journaling, whatever it is you can spark fun in your creative mind.

- Cultivate new friendships

- Don't bother trying to figure out if he is truly a narcissist, misunderstood, or a jerk. If he is any of these, you need to turn and run!

- Don't engage with him, or his flying monkeys. They are who they are. Anyone who believes them is not worth your time.

- Dream big

- Educate yourself on something for your greater purpose, or for fun!

- Elevate yourself

- EFT – Emotional Freedom Technique is a powerful tool to practice helping soothe and calm stress.

- Empowerment – the narcissist hates empowerment. Of course, I do not recommend any type of revenge. Going no contact and empowerment are the only revenge you will have against your narcissist.

- Fix and heal yourself

- Feed yourself with quality food, quality activities, and quality thoughts. You are quality. You deserve the best!

- Forgive yourself

- Focus on the good events, people, and things in your life and surroundings.

- Fun – have it, embrace it (it's okay to have fun! Give yourself permission to have fun!)

- Get clear about your life! (Goals, vision, decision, people you want in your life, be deliberate)

- Get help in deactivating triggers and taking the charge from them

- Grace – You have grace. Always remember that.

- Gratitude – You must incorporate appreciation, being thankful into all aspects of your life. The more gratitude you have for all things around you, the more you will have an awesome life. Every day find three reasons you are grateful.

- Gratitude journal

- Healing – nothing to fear

- Help others – I found this has been critical to healing.

- Higher power – Believe in something: God, Jesus, the Universe, Allah, Buddha, angels, whatever. You will find strength in faith.

■ Hypnotherapy – This helps reduce and often eliminate stress.

■ Intentions – Create a goal each day. Create goals, intentions many times a day.

■ Intuition

■ Inspire others with your story of empowerment!

■ Journaling – This is incredibly helpful.

■ Know yourself

■ Knowledge

■ Laugh – laugh a lot!

■ Learn – learn –and keep learning

■ Love – Surround yourself with things YOU love, people you love/enjoy/love you.

■ Love yourself

■ Mastermind groups are helpful in reaching your goals.

■ Mindfulness Meditation

■ Minimize the damage

■ Motivation – Increase your motivation by setting goals, following through with the work needed to accomplish them. Don't give up!

■ NLP – Neuro Linguistic Programming will help you increase the positivity in your life. NLP changes the negative chatter in your mind to thoughts of empowerment.

■ No reaction

■ Observant – Notice your thoughts – be observant to your inner conversation. Make sure your thoughts and inner dialogs are positive!

■ Pamper yourself

■ Personal development

■ Positivity – Surround yourself with positive people and things that make you happy.

■ Power – You have unlimited potential in having your own personal power!

■ Protection – Protect yourself against flying monkeys, abuse by proxy, and the unexpected by having a coping plan of action prepared.

■ Read

■ Receive authentic love from others and from yourself

■ Redirect your thoughts

■ Remove yourself from negativity, negative situations, and negative people.

■ Restore faith in yourself

■ Revitalize yourself

■ Rewrite your personal story – It's amazing!

■ Seek help from experts and specialists

- Self-esteem

- Self-worth – YOU ARE WORTH ALL GOOD THINGS! YOU ARE AWESOME!

- Set goals

- Share your story – don't be ashamed

- Solutions

- Stress management

- SUPPORT! Get lots of support! Mastermind groups are awesome!

- Surround yourself with awesome, supportive people. Give all others the gift of "goodbye."

- Take action – Set some new goals and take action towards achieving them.

- Triggers – There will be triggers that pop up unexpectedly.

- Trust yourself/Trust your inner voice

- Unfollowing the narcissist's rules – The narcissist has irrational, constantly changing rules you are expected to adhere. While you are with the narcissist, or have recently left him, or have recently been ghosted by the narcissist, you need to unfollow those crazymaking rules immediately.

- Visualize your successful day each morning. Visualize your successful life! Visualization gives you direction. You are going places!

- Volunteer – find your passion

- You have choices!

- You are not alone!

#abusersabuse

NATIONAL DOMESTIC ABUSE HOTLINE
1-800-799-7233

"I Love You" From The Perspective Of A Narcissist
By Tin Nước Hàn- July 14, 2018

Dear Codependent Partner,

I will never say these words to you in reality because if I did it would reveal how I deliberately exploit the world for the only thing I care about—my benefit. Since I only care about myself, I need you to carry all the load of the relationship while I reap the benefits of it.

When I say I love you, I really do mean it though. I love how hard you work for me. I love that I have forced you to compromise on everything to keep me happy. I love that you do everything for me but you have given up expecting me to return that courtesy.

I love that I have the power to reduce you to tears, make you feel small and insignificant, and gloat about how powerful that makes me feel. I know you let me walk over you, and I keep pulling you down so that you don't realize you deserve a lot better than what I give you.

I love how I can blame you for gas-lighting or just call you crazy when you bring up things I don't want to discuss. Also, I love that I can keep expecting more and more from you while you keep lowering your expectations of me. It makes my life so easy when you let me walk all over you!

I love how I can take your innocence and kindness for granted, using it for my thrill and pleasure. I love how I can always keep all your focus on alleviating my pain and discomfort. Nothing ever is enough; I don't feel loved enough, respected, admired and cared for enough. And all of this misery I dump on you to fix.

It is not that I don't know that you need support, love, and care; I just don't think it is as important as my feelings. I am the priority for the both of us, and that is really all I want. It is never about the closeness, empathy or connection you want. It is never about how I hurt you. It is always about how I can control you and make you feel like you are not doing enough.

I am superior to you, and I love you as one loves a precious possession. You are just like all the other nice things I want to own and I love the envy others feel when they see you on my arm.

Since I am constantly hurting others, my brain suffers from self-loathing 24/7. This is why I love spending time with you. I love feeding off your emotional support, and I love hating you for needing you constantly. I love blaming you for my own narcissistic tendencies.

I love you because I am scared and tired of the self-loathing inside me. All the feelings I am too scared to have, the neediness, the emotions, everything I call you weak and crazy for, makes me love you because I feed off of you. I love you because I can treat you like a punching bag when that deep weak part of me threatens to open up. You keep all of it at bay and I take you for granted because I hate that I need you as much as I do.

Of course the day you realize all of this, you will leave me. So, I will never tell you, and I will always keep you hoping that I will become a better person, but in reality, I never will. Only if you walk away from me, will my complacency ever get displaced. The day you stop caring, I will fall and I will learn my lesson. Yet I know that day will never come because I keep you so tangled up in my concerns that you can never think about yours. And that is just perfect for me.

With my endless self-love,

Your Narcissist Other.

WORK CITED

American Psychiatric Association. (2013). *Diagnostic and statistical manual of mental disorders: DSM-5* (5th ed.). Arlington, VA: American Psychiatric Association.

Han, Tin Nuroc (2018, July 14). "'I Love You' From the Perceptive of a Narcissist." Retrieved from http://tinnuochan.com/i-love-you-from-the-perspective-of-a-narcissist/

Hoffer, Michelle (2017), *Soaring Minds*. Mechanicsburg, PA: Sunbury Press.

SOARING MINDS:
EMPOWERING LIVES. HEALING SOULS.

A message to you:

Soaring Minds, and The Soaring Minds System is intended to show you how to awaken the power within you, teach you how to heal to become empowered.

Using The Soaring Minds System will help you strengthen your connection to your purpose, your higher power, and will help you improve your self-confidence, and self-love.

Soaring Minds Workbook and Journal will give you an overall sampling of the lessons and work you need to do to go from a sad and dire state to one of purpose, authentic happiness, and joy. It will aid in your recovery from narcissistic abuse.

Look for the following workbooks and journals in the Soaring Minds System:

Soaring Minds Workbook and Journal

Soaring with Forgiveness

Soaring with Gratitude

Soaring with Faith

Soaring with Love

Soaring with the Law of Attraction

As well as:

The ABCs of Narcissism

The ABCs of Narcissism – A Guide for Him

www.SoaringMinds.me

Email Michelle Williard Hoffer at Michelle@SoaringMInds.me

Follow on Facebook: Soaring Minds

Twitter: @Soaring_Minds

Instagram: Michelle Williard Hoffer

#abusersabuse   #soaringminds

Made in the USA
San Bernardino,
CA